Testimony and Witnessing in Psychoanalysis

In this fascinating volume, Zipi Rosenberg Schipper approaches the fundamental topic of testimony, seeking to recognize its value as a distinct and vital function in psychoanalytic work, separate from its inherited importance to work on trauma.

Rosenberg Schipper introduces a revivifying philosophical, linguistic and psychoanalytic approach to the act of testimony, focusing on the role of witnessing in daily life and the importance it has as a therapeutic tool in psychoanalytic and psychological therapy. Throughout, she pinpoints three key psychoanalytic theories on patient testimony. She begins by looking at Freud's foundational work on testimony as a means of concealing the unconscious and the questions of credibility in the consulting room this creates before looking at Winnicottian and Kohutian theories, whereby therapists take everything the patient says as a definitive truth. She concludes by looking at the Intersubjective and Relational schools of thought, where the therapist assumes the role of witness.

By providing a comprehensive overview of the conflicting theories on the topic, Rosenberg Schipper equips practicing psychoanalysts and analysts-in-training with the tools necessary to utilize this vital therapeutic device and engage with it in treatment for all patients.

Zipi Rosenberg Schipper is a clinical psychologist, supervisor and occupational therapist working in private practice in Tel Aviv, Israel.

Testimony and Witnessing in Psychoanalysis

A Literary and Philosophical Perspective

Zipi Rosenberg Schipper

Routledge
Taylor & Francis Group

LONDON AND NEW YORK

Designed cover image: Cover Image by Dan Rosenberg

First published 2024
by Routledge
4 Park Square, Milton Park, Abingdon, Oxon OX14 4RN

and by Routledge
605 Third Avenue, New York, NY 10158

Routledge is an imprint of the Taylor & Francis Group, an informa business

British Library Cataloguing-in-Publication Data
A catalogue record for this book is available from the British Library

ISBN: 978-1-032-51783-4 (hbk)
ISBN: 978-1-032-51780-3 (pbk)
ISBN: 978-1-003-40392-0 (ebk)

DOI: 10.4324/9781003403920

Typeset in Times New Roman
by Apex CoVantage, LLC

To My Mother
Whom I witnessed so little

Contents

Acknowledgment

To those who have helped me to learn the power of testimony.

Credit Lines

Prof Rafi Weichert, Editor-in-Chief, Keshev Publishing House permission to use a quote from *"The Rhyme of the Ancient Mariner"* by S.T Coleridge, holding the copyrights for the Hebrew translation.

Moshe Vidal Advocate, Administrator of Pinchas Sade Estate, and **Ms. Eilat Negev and Mr. Yehuda Koren,** authors, editors of Pinchas Sade's *"Diaries"*. Permission to cite from *"Diaries"* of Pinchas Sade, 2014

Warren Poland, permission to deliberately to cite from his article: "The Analyst's Witnessing and Otherness", 2000.

Linda Mark, Journals Production Editor, Guilford Publications permission to cite 2 from: Seiden, H.M. (1996). "The Healing Presence"

Yael Hadass, General Manager Schocken Publishing House permission to cite from the poem by Yehuda Amichai, from his book *"Open Closed Open"*.

Dvora Levinger, Mosad Bialik permission to cite from *"Essays in First Person"*, by Aharon Appelfeld. The Zionist Library, Jerusalem

Kochava Kamir, Yuda Atlas, Keter Press, Jerusalem Permission given to cite the poem: "Far from Home", *"This Child is Me"* (1977).

Kochava Kamir, Keter Press, Jerusalem, permission to cite from *"Labyrinth"*, Borges 1960

Itai Weiss, Am Oved Press, permission to cite from Kafka's *"Octavo Notes."*

Hani Ahrony, Bar-Ilan University, permission to cite from Avi Sagi's book: *"The Human Voyage to Meaning – A philosophical – Hermeneutical study of Literary Works"* (2009).

Dan Rosenberg, photographer, permission to use his image in the front cover of the book.

Forward – Introductory by Prof. Avi Sagi

The question of the significance of oral testimony is a subject featured again and again in contemporary research literature.

For the most part, the analysis of testimony relates mostly to its contents, whereas Dr. Rosenberg Schipper's work focuses on analyzing the act of testimony itself. Her analysis shows that the act of testimony is an expression of the presence of both the testifier and the recipient. The latter's presence and attendance are reflected by the concern and care shown by the recipient towards the testifier.

The book is divided into two parts:

The first part of the book – "What is Spoken Testimony", investigates the essence and meaning of testimony as it is expressed in prose, poetry, social culture and philosophy and psychoanalysis.

The second part – "Testimony as a Therapeutic Function in Psychoanalysis and Psychotherapy" – offers a new perspective of the meaning of testimony in the clinical field, which is expressed in three contexts:

First, the book challenges the view of testimony through the prism of trauma, adopted by the world of psychology, which regards the importance of testimony solely in terms of its efficacy in the treatment of trauma and thereby misses its other significant clinical aspects. The book calls for a reformulation of the role of testimony as a means of psychic change in every therapy.

In the second context, the book draws attention to the fact that both the therapist and the patient are witnesses, even though in the psychoanalytic discourse, the references are associated only with the therapist as a witness.

In the third context, the book draws, for the first time, technical and clinical characteristics of the therapist and the patient as witnesses.

In this part, the book consists of a detailed review of the writings of psychoanalytic researchers on the subject of testimony in therapy.

Zipi Rosenberg Schipper's book is an original and significant contribution to the discourse on testimony and opens up new horizons for the analysis of this important and interesting phenomenon.

I was always looking for a witness for life. This is what I always wanted,
Without him it is not possible.
Maybe it is possible to live without a witness, and always continue to look for
*   him and hope . . .*
A witness is the sign of our being alive here, on earth.
Even in death, testimony is important.

"The Diaries", Pinchas Sadeh (2014) [2]

Preface

At a psychology conference held in the beautiful city of Cambridge, I hung a poster depicting the role of testimony in psychotherapy. The display was in a spacious, brightly lit room. As I hung the poster and straightened the corners, I wondered whether I had chosen a good place and whether anyone would even show an interest, and I did not notice that a woman was standing in front of the poster staring at it with fixed eyes. She stood there motionless for a few minutes, her eyes filled with tears and muttering: **"so true, so true"**.

She then wiped her tears away and left.
People approached, asked questions, a discussion began . . . But I waited for her to return.
Only late that evening, she came back.
"I learned how important testimony is when I was in therapy", she said and added:

> My therapist was the only witness to my life, she witnessed my secret experiences, my difficulty in starting treatment, in being a mother or parting from Mom . . . the enormous pain I felt when she died, was as if all the things she had witnessed went with her

This story reflects what the phenomenon of testimony and witnessing is all about.

Parents witness their children, children witness their parents, as do caregivers, teachers, friends, neighbors, therapists and patients. Witnessing is a phenomenon of "Being with". Growing up without a witness leads to difficult situations of loneliness.

Testimony is part of our existence. It is an everyday phenomenon that constantly accompanies us but is taken for granted and is only felt when absent. Nevertheless, it has not gained interest in academic research. Even Greek mythology, which created gods for almost every worldly phenomenon, did not honor testimony with a god or a goddess of its own.

Today, things have changed, and testimony is viewed as deserving its own god/goddess. It seems that in Delphi, the ancient gateway, where the words "Know thy self" are engraved, this maxim should be replaced by the inscription "Be thy self".[1] And in order to be ourselves, we need witnesses around us.

I have learned the power of testimony and witnessing at the clinic.

The will to investigate the function of testimony was born when I was a young professional practitioner, and it has been reinforced in the years since, despite the lack of interest in psychoanalytic theory or in all the various training courses I engaged in.

A similar gap also exists in daily life, where on the one hand, we are, to a large extent, dependent on the testimonies of others; their epistemological position was, and remains, controversial.

This is the lacuna into which this book has entered in an attempt to see the act of testimony as a whole show and, by that, to build a bridge between the level of deeds and the theoretical level.

This intends to bring about proper recognition of testimony's status and to locate it in an appropriate place among the list of the key psychoanalytic functions.

Towards the end of the 20th century, a paradigmatic turn has taken place, and from an action measured by the information it provides, it has been recognized as a medium of healing. This turning point found prominent expression first in the field of the arts, chiefly in literature and cinema, and only later did it enter the fields of philosophy and psychoanalysis.

Testimony is usually examined according to the contents expressed in it, while this book examines the actual act of testimony itself and focuses on its roles in daily life and in the therapeutic field.

This book is focused on two dimensions of testimony: The epistemological status of spoken testimony and the perspective of being present of witnessing.

Every testimony encompasses at least three testimonies. One tells of the narrator's experience; the second is the testimony heard by the recipient, which necessarily differs from that of the narrator; and there is the third one – the witness's inner testimony, unknown to anyone other than the witness himself, and which nobody else other than him, feels. It is an inner experience, which, from the moment it turns into words, it changes.

In recent years the desire for witnesses has become extreme, principally in social media. This is a global trend that seeks witnesses to every conceivable matter. The demand for privacy, which had been so dominant in Western society, has been put aside, and today there is a mass craving for witnesses.

What is it about testimony that succeeds in binding such contradictions and such forces?

This book investigates this question, and it is the first of three books dealing with spoken testimony. The present book is divided into two parts: Part 1 examines the essence of the phenomenon from a philosophical and literary perspective. Part 2 describes how this essence constitutes a significant therapeutic tool in psychoanalytical or psychological therapy and specifies the roles of witnessing in our lives.

The second book illustrates the roles of testimony and witnessing in an individual's life through stories of testimony from the Clinique. The third book relates to Paul Celan's statement – said when awarded the Bremen Literature Prize (1958): "Each poem is a testimony".[2]

Notes

1 In 1891, Oscar Wilde suggested that instead of the inscription "Know yourself" engraved on the gates to the world at Delphi, it should be substituted with the inscription "Be yourself". In order to be ourselves we need witnesses who see us.
2 Celan, Paul (1950): *Selected Poems and Prose of Paul Celan.* W. W. Norton & Co. Inc, Hakibuts Hameuchad Publishing House, Bnei Brak, Israel (1997), p. 126 (Hebrew).

Part 1

What Is Spoken Testimony

Chapter 1

What Are We Talking About When Discussing Spoken Testimony?

Zipi Rosenberg Schipper

What Is Spoken Testimony?

Spoken Testimony is, first of all, an act of speech. It is the delivery of the witness' words which are basically addressed to an-other. Without both, it has no existence. This resembles the philosophical question posed by George Berkeley (1710), "If there was a sound when a tree fell down in a forest and there was no one there to hear it".[1]

The concept of spoken testimony is elusive since its borders are not entirely sealed. It is difficult to investigate it because speech, which is its main component, is a variable that cannot be completely isolated. Every act of speech is dependent on the speaker, and every speech is a speech about something, and the three are inseparable.

John L. Austin's philosophical-philological model suggests that spoken testimony is an "Illocutionary act".[2] This maxim means that the act of speech is expressed in the act itself. The act is not thought of as reaching the level of the ultimate validation of its contents. According to Austin, this facilitates a perspective that accords a place to a more formally phrased speech or a simple daily statement that is also true of both first-hand and hearsay testimony.

However, it is clear that the phenomenon of spoken testimony is much more than that and that all the formal and informal definitions do not exhaust its full meaning. For example, defining it as an 'illocutionary expression' does not differentiate it from other communicative acts, such as a promise, or a warning, or a report or an order.[3]

The ontological aspect of the phenomenon, according to which the deliverance of testimony is a binding framework between addressor and recipient, distinguishes it from other social acts. But even so, the ontological aspect alone also doesn't exhaust the full meaning of testimony.

If the definitions weave in an additional discourse, it is more often than not the judicial discourse. In daily use, the spoken testimony does not contain existential or psychological connotations and, in a natural way, relates to information given by witnesses in court. It would appear that the principal reason for this is that the word 'testimony' barely appears in daily or social situations, in philosophical lectures or in therapeutic narratives.

DOI: 10.4324/9781003403920-2

In their book "*Testimony: The Crisis of Witnessing in Literature, Psychoanalysis, and History*" (1992), Shoshana Felman and Dori Laub drew up general guidelines as to how testimony should be defined:[4]

- "To testify . . . is to accomplish a speech act, rather than to simply formulate a statement."[5]
- "In the legal philosophical and tradition of the Western world, witnessing is based on, and is formally defined by, first-hand seeing. 'Eyewitness testimony' is what constitutes the most decisive law of evidence in courtrooms."[6]
- "To testify – to vow to tell, to promise and produce one's own speech as material evidence for truth – is to accomplish a speech act."[7]

The emphasis on the words "to accomplish a speech act" in the first and third definitions points to the difficulty of creating spoken testimony. Indeed, spoken testimony has a rhythm of its own that interweaves speech and silence. The spoken version is formed in the process and occasionally begins with the absence of any version whatsoever.

Giving testimony has a timetable of its own. It moves through time in opposite directions. It always starts at the end of the story. As Sagi (2009) puts it: "The story of testimony supports the present, and such a support both biases and constructs the past."[8]

The word 'testimony' has a double meaning.[9] In one sense, it refers to an event that took place at a given time in an individual's life (giving testimony) that sometimes has a point effect and sometimes constitutes the course of life. This refers to a real event that the addresser witnessed, which, after it occurred, became an inner experience.

The second meaning is the verbalization of the event (bearing witness). This is the second stage of the process of testimony that takes place in the present, recounting the 'event' in the past. The inner experience is made public by verbalizing it in front of a listening witness.

The role of the recipient is to allow the testimony to come into being. This second stage validates the inner experience, and by that, the testimony gets different status on the part of the narrator, making it easier to cope with.

A testimony's space is, therefore, a space of an activity that has still not been conceptualized and is not anchored in any existing philosophical or psychoanalytic theory. It appears to be more a matter of an action than of a theory.

The Sources of Testimony

All the Sources of Testimony are anchored in the Holy Scriptures.

The word 'testimony' in the Torah (Hebrew Bible) holds an especially honorable place and is likened to the Torah as a whole.

The '*Tablets of the Law*' are also known as the 'Tablets of Testimony'.

Three verses teach us about the esteem of testimony as analogous to the whole of the Bible and as representing the covenant between Man and God:

- *"And thou shalt give unto the ark the testimony which I shall give unto thee"* (Exodus 25: 16).
- *"And thou shalt give the atonement unto the ark from above, and unto the ark shalt thou give the testimony which I shall give thee"* (Exodus 25:21).
- When Moses came down from mount Sinai, he held the two *"tables of the testimony"* (Exodus 34:29).

The Holy Bible is also called 'The New Testament', and the term testimony is derived from it.

Witnesses in the Tanakh (the five books of Moses, Prophets and scriptures) play a role in treaties between nations and, in this sense, also serve as a 'Third Force'; though it is not a partner to such treaties, in its absence, the event would not be considered valid.[10]

Testimony touches on the interrelationship between Man and God and talks of a continuous and protective guarding presence. Testimony in the Bible also relates to prophecy, and in that sense, it encompasses both mysticism and holiness.

All these meanings are characteristic of the act of testimony and especially that of personal testimony, in biblical times as well as today.

Personal testimony is the testimony of an individual about himself. Historically, this notion is based on the martyr, who personified the witness of faith, willing to sacrifice his own body in order to affirm his religious beliefs.

Despite the passage of time, the phenomenon of the martyr has left its deep imprint on the image of personal testimony to this day.

Most of the verses of the testimony in the Bible are legal laws. The laws of witnessing and testimony are determinations of what is and is not legally permissible. They are the raw material for many of the laws of testimony that appear in the Halakha, in the Mishnah and the Talmud.

The sages delved deeply into those verses of testimony in the Bible and interpreted them from different angles. Their interpretations covered a very broad range of issues, giving the witness and his testimony a great deal of power in legal procedures and are used to validate information on issues of a wide range of areas of life: property laws, marriage and divorce laws, family laws and social laws – between man and his friend, between man and himself and between man and God. All of these constitute, to this day, the basis for the treatment of spoken testimony, first in the 'Hebrew law' and later in the 'Israeli law'.

The Ontology of Spoken Testimony

There are three entities in the act of testimony: the addresser, the addressee and the spoken testimony.

Between the three entities, there is a hierarchy of importance.

Heading the pyramid is the spoken testimony itself, which is at the heart of the phenomenon rather than the meeting between the two. This is contrary to what is generally accepted in most social practices, including the therapeutic situation, where the encounter relationship created between patient and therapist is what matters.

The story of testimony is the real thing and has more power than even the individual delivering it, like a good performance transcending the actor or a good book transcending the author.

One of the most prominent writers who related to the subject of speech was the French phenomenological philosopher Merleau M. Ponty (1964), who noted that:

> A thinking which looks on from above, and thinks of the object-in-general, must return to the "there is" (il y a), which underlies it; to the site, the soil of the sensible and opened world such as it is in our life and for our body – not that possible body which we may legitimately think of as an information machine but that actual body I call mine, this sentinel standing quietly at the command of my words and my acts.[11]

Next in the hierarchy of importance is the deliverer of the testimony, who has greater power than the 'other' who is listening, because he had direct contact with the real, with the thing itself. **He was there!**

Though the addressee is third in rank, it is he, ironically, who enables the existence of the testimony. It is his presence that allows the situation to occur. In giving testimony, the person talks to the other and, at the same time, talks to himself.

A 'good' witness puts his own needs and the color with which he is accustomed to painting his world aside and allows the testimony to exist.

The key words of the phenomenon of spoken testimony are **trust** and **being present**.

Martin Buber, in his book "*I and Thou*" (1923), conducts a debate with this presence, which, in his view, has three components: mutuality, acceptance and contact connection.

In Buber's words

> What (the testifier) man receives is not a "content" but a presence, a presence as strength. This presence and strength, includes three elements that are not separate, but may nevertheless be contemplated as three. First, the whole abundance of actual reciprocity, of being admitted, of being associated while one is altogether unable to indicate what that is like with which one is associated, nor does association make life any easier for us – it makes life heavier.[12]

The model of interpersonal relationships developed by Sagi (2012), the existence of personal testimony is conditioned by the "Ethics of presence", also termed "Ethics of self-withdrawal".[13] Sagi delineates the characteristic aspects that typify the position of the recipient and argues that the necessary condition for the existence of documentation (documentation=testimony) is the transition of the receiver of testimony from ethics of sovereignty to ethics of presence.

Sagi notes:

> The withdrawal into the self means that the sovereign has to retreat into his inwardness, suspends his activity, and focuses on a position of openness and attentiveness to the other. . . . As a result, he is open to what is in front of him.[14]

One can therefore say that the situation of testimony differs from other verbal acts such as – promising, reporting, warning, ordering or even blessing – in the reciprocal relations between the three entities in the situation: the testimony, the addresser and the addressee. These relations lead to a unique form of mutuality.

The Structure of Testimony

The various acts of testimony share a common idea, and the structure of all of them is similar. Indeed, in all verbal testimonies and in all the contexts – in courts of law and in social, historical and personal testimonies – the testimony always recounts what had happened to the addressor. Thus, a basic pattern is woven, the essence of which is, "We are here to hear about the event as you have witnessed it".

Testimony as a structure is 'indifferent' to the contents that pass through it. Therefore, despite the contradictory contexts, the basic structure is a kind of **line** connecting two people with mutual relations or an individual and a group.

Addressor_____Addressee

However, an ontological view reveals a triangle of beings in the structure of testimony, between which there are reciprocal relations: the witness who testifies, the testimony and the witness who observes and listens, becoming a witness to the witness.

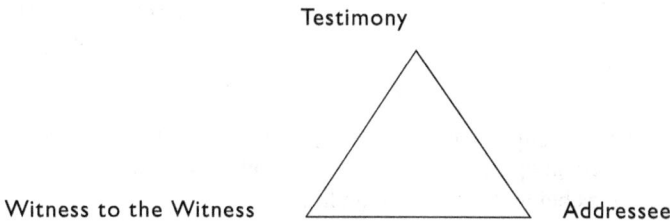

Testimony

Witness to the Witness   Addressee

And yet, this triangle of forces doesn't fully describe testimony because testimony is given in a variety of contexts, and every spoken text has its context. One cannot talk of testimony without talking about the discourse.[15] The discourse is the context, and the meaning changes accordingly. The comprehensive diagram would therefore be a form consisting of four vertices in which, between them in every direction, there are reciprocal relations.

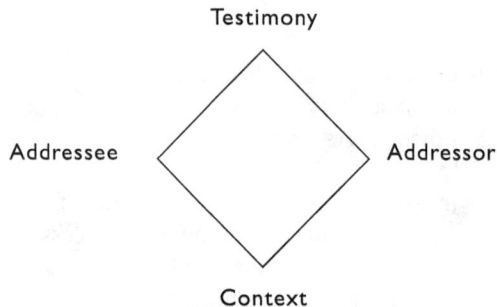

Testimony

Addressee   Addressor

Context

Every variety of testimony has a similar structure. However, in practice, the situation of testimony has a number of layers that have different meanings in differing contexts. When each one of these situations is deconstructed, the differences become evident from three points of view:

- The importance attached to the value of the truth of the testimony.
- The emotional meaning of the testimony to the addressee and the addressor.
- The reason for giving the testimony.

These three differences in meaning touch upon two of the major philosophical questions that the phenomenon of testimony corresponds to:

- The question of certainty.
- The question of the other.

The Components of Testimony: Speech

> *Humans create, dream, fail, imagine and act through words, which is sometimes a continuous text and sometimes is a meaningful silence. Man is made in speech and by speech.*
> **Sagi, Avi** (2009)[16]

The act of speech is the main component of spoken testimony. Speech is the unique way in which a person approaches an-other. The other is another, who is separate from him as well as being the other within him.

Ferdinand de Saussure (1916) an innovative philologist, was the first to distinguish between language (*Langue*) and speech. In this classical differentiation of his, he regarded language as "language without speech".[17] He noted: "Linguistic structure . . . is the whole set of linguistic signs which enables one to understand

and to make himself understood."[18] Meaning that language is a general system and speaking is a private one.

Speech is the way of expressing consciousness, and in fact, without words, we have no consciousness. Conscious thinking is distinguished from unconscious thought, in that the person says it to himself or to an-other.[19]

This understanding depicts speech as an act that accepts being beyond what is seen or heard. That is to say, speech is a conditional variable conditioned by the speaker and just as there is conscious and unconscious awareness, so too speech can be conscious and unconscious.

The act of speaking, including the act of spoken testimony, has a double meaning. "On the one hand the action of speech is an action of a verb, and on the other hand, speech is always turned on an object."[20] These resemble two pages glued together that cannot be separated.

Analyzing the meaning of speech can thus be achieved, both in reference to the verb and also through reference to the object. For example, speech as contemplation aloud indicates the verb aspect, and calling the thing by name belongs to the object aspect.

The Dominance of Eye Witnessing in the Act of Testimony

The evidence of an eyewitness occupies a preferential position in the judicial history of the act of testimony.[21]

In the discussion of the subject of the relations between testimony, narrative and history, Felman and Laub (1992) refer to the importance status of the eyewitness.

> Joining events to language, the narrator-as-eyewitness is the testimonial bridge which, mediating between narrative and history, guarantees their correspondence and adherence to each other.[22]

There is an enlightening example in a biblical story; it is to be found in the chapter about the "Tower of Babel" – the "Sailing Generation", in which it is told about a move made by God: "*The Lord came down to see the city and the tower the people were building*" (Geneses 5:11)

There is a further example during the period when the fate of the people of Sodom and Gomorrah was being decided: "And the Lord said: *I'll go down and see whether they have done altogether according to the outcry that has come to me; and if not, I will know.*" (Genesis 18:21).

The question arises: What reason was there for God's descent? It is a question already asked in the *Old Midrash Tanchuma*: "*and the Lord descended in order to see.*"[23] The answer is that, of course, the descent was not really necessary but "came to teach judges not to convict until they see for themselves, and understand."[24]

Having said all of that, we put into doubt[25] that a deep analysis of the act of eye witnessing doesn't, in any way, provide us with epistemological certainty. Seeing is not a purely sensory phenomenon, nor is it entirely conscious.

Ludwig Wittgenstein pointed out that seeing is not a clear-cut variable and that, at times, it is misleading.

In his words:

I say there is a chair . . . it suddenly disappears . . . so it wasn't a chair but some kind of illusion.[26]

And in another place:

The one man might make an accurate drawing of the two faces, and the other notice in the drawing the likeness, which the former did not see.[27]

And also:

Do I really see something else every time, or am I interpreting what I see in a different way? I prefer the first one, but why? To interpret means to think, to do something, seeing is a situation.[28]

Martin Heidegger (1962) also pointed to the gap between what is seen by the eye and the thing itself: "What appears does not show itself; and anything which thus fails to show itself, is also something which can be seen."[29]

Also, in *"The Origin of the Act of Art"* by Heidegger (1935): "Seeing what appears . . . is based on sight . . . but does not mean just perceiving with the bodily eyes, but neither does it mean pure no sensory awareness".[30]

A classic corroboration of the claim that eye witnessing is entirely subjective is evidenced in the prize-winning movie *"Rashomon"* (1950), produced by the Japanese Director Akira Kurosawa, which is a perfect example of the illusions of seeing and their influence on spoken testimony.

The movie is based on two stories by the Japanese writer Ryūnosuke Akutagawa, describing crimes of rape and murder through the eyes of four eyewitnesses: the accused of rape and murder, the murdered person, the raped woman and a woodcutter who was an eyewitness to what had happened. The four testimonies contradict each other, and the observer is unable to discover the truth and receives no answers as to the circumstances of the death. The murder and the rape are objective givens, but the description of the circumstances surrounding them are entirely subjective and reflect the personal interpretation given by each of the witnesses.

An additional point is the fact that eye witnessing is not exactly a matter external to the event itself, which it often is thought to be. The witness's act of watching the incident is part of the event itself and influences it.

The History of the Meaning of Speech

For hundreds of years of philosophical thought, language expressed a connection between thought and reality rather than interpersonal relations. As Gadamer (2004) put it:

> In the earliest times the intimate unity of word and thing, was so obvious that the true name was considered to be part of the bearer of the name, if not indeed to substitute for him. In Greek the expression for "word", oncome, also means "name", and especially "proper name" – i.e., the name by which something is called. The word is understood primarily as a name. But a name is what it is because it is what someone is called and what he answers to. It belongs to its bearer. The rightness of the name is confirmed by the fact that someone answers

In other words, the general philosophical perception of the phenomenon of speech was determined for centuries as an expression of consciousness, like a vocalized contemplation, thought or conveying an idea. All of which are monologic sayings, a saying which doesn't await a response.

A talk between two people was perceived in the past as a malfunction or as a tool to acquire things. Indeed, few thinkers in the history of philosophy saw speech as a seminal moment in a person's life. Mikhail Bakhtin (1960) formulated it thus:

> Several other versions of the function of language have been and are now being suggested, but it is still typical to underestimate, if not altogether ignore, the communicative function of language. Language is regarded from the speaker's standpoint as if there were only one speaker who does not have any necessary relation to other participants in speech communication.[31]

The perception of speech as a communicative tool, that combines a framework of addressor and addressee, is a relatively new concept, formed only towards the end of the 19th century[32] and more so at the beginning of the 20th century, not least because of the development of psychoanalysis and the works of philosophical-philological researchers who focused on the act of speech such as De Saussure (1916), Roland Barthes (2006) and Franz Rosenzweig (1916), and also Heidegger's "Linguistic Concept" (1978), as well as his book *"The Basic Problems of Phenomenology"* (1982).

A fine example of the development of speech from a monologue to an approach to an-other is the narrative of the Biblical book of Genesis. The first embodiment of speech in the story of creation is speech as an act: *"And God said, let there be light, and there was light."* (Genesis 1:3). However, in the first story of Genesis, a different aspect of speech is already revealed, akin to a reflection or a forethought: *"And God said, Let there be a firmament in the midst of the waters, and let it divide the waters from the waters"* (Genesis 1:6–7).

A forethought is also to be found in the story of the creation of Man: "*And God said: Let us make man in our image, after our likeness*" (Genesis 1:26). It resembles the creation of the sky, but there is a difference.

Sagi (2009) explains:

> In the creation of the sky, speech was imperative – "*And God said, Let there be a firmament in the midst of the waters*" (Genesis 1, 6) while in the creation of man the speech is reflective and projective, i.e. future-oriented, meaning that the turn in speech takes place regarding man only. There is not yet a dialogic speech, but there is a mirror picture between the first man and God.[33]

The dialogue appears in the conversation between God and Abraham, in the Chapter of Sodom: "*Wilt Thou indeed sweep away the righteous with the wicked?*" (Genesis 18:22), and God answered him: "*And the Lord said: if I find in Sodom fifty righteous within the city, then I will forgive all the place for the sake*" (26).

"God's response to Abraham is the profound expression of the power of dialogue – which is the power to change."[34]

How Does It Actually Happen?

The inevitable question is, "How Does it Actually Happen?" Or, how does the experience pass on from Addressor to Addressee?

Research of the act of speech and its implications has difficulty explaining the question of the link between speech and its object or the question of the relation between the space of speech and the space of the object of speech.

Ferdinand De Saussure (1916) suggested a theoretical framework that deals with the essence of the concept of 'language'. He developed the important distinction between the signifier, which is the acoustic imagery that is the spoken word, and the signified, which is the object of the speech and argued that the relationship between them was arbitrary.

Roland Barthes (1967), on the other hand, regarded semiology as part of philology. He claimed that the objects of the language are always linguistic objects – whether it is the signified or the signifier. According to him: "The objects of a language cannot exist in the world that is external to the language."[35]

These two linguistic theories that made a huge contribution to the study of language and speech miss the 'element of the bridging' that is built at the time of spoken testimony between addressor and addressee.

A fitting answer to the question is to be found in Heidegger's linguistic views in Heidegger (1971) as well as Heidegger (1947), informing us about the link between consciousness and speech and its object.

According to him we live at the language, "Language is the house of being."[36]

Heidegger honored speech and the spoken words more than the written. According to him, "Language is presented in terms of speech, in the sense of sounds",[37] "and the voices present the desires of the mind."[38]

Meaning that the spoken word is what enables the information to become known. Speech does not represent the occurrence but presents it and, in that sense, also animates it. In spoken testimony, the addressor invites the addressee to recognize the experience of the event in question, "and even if the recipient can never experience what happened", Heidegger argues, "the power that was in it, passes to the recipient who is there".[39]

That is to say, that speech is a space of presence; it shows something and allows it to be. In this way, the experience passes from the addressor to the addressee and changes its status in both of them. "Consciousness collects memories and speech animates them with the help of the imagination".[40]

Monologue versus Dialogue

In a monologue, there is just one party that tells his story. It is based on a clear hierarchy, assumes the existence of one certainty and doesn't lead to a response from those present.[41]

In a dialogue, there is an approach to an-other and the receipt of a response from him. In this, there is a degree of risk. No one can be sure in advance what will 'come out' of a conversation. The danger is that the other will teach her/him something about her/his existence. This power is the power of change, which is also the therapeutic power.

Franz Rosenzweig (1921)[42] distinguishes between the monologic philosophical thought and the practical dialogue. "The philosophy of Rozenzweig", writes Yehoyada Amir in the introduction to Rozenzweig's book (1921), "teaches a person to rely on what he knows and experiences. Rosenzweig disagrees with what had been the accepted way of thought and claims that the denial of a realistic life experience negates, or at best, lessens, what is said by an-other.

He writes:

From its very beginning and until the 19th century, philosophy mislead mankind by promises of "fake magic", if only it would agree to leave the Platonic "cave" and recognize that everything experienced in real life, is nothing other than a false perception. The denial of the experience of the realistic life of a person who lives and works in the world is the basis of the failure concealed in philosophy.[43] Rozenzweig's view, reality is not based on an idea but is the continuous encounter between speech and its foundations: God, world and man.

Is Testimony Simulacra?

The term 'simulacra' was coined by Jean Baudrillard (1981). The origin of the word is Latin and means an image or representation of someone or something or a nonexistent entity. Simulation is the appearance of something as actual with the intent of creating an illusion of its reality, as opposed to the simulator that imagines a certain origin. Baudrillard's Simulacra "is the generation by models of a real, without origin or reality: a hyperreal".[44] "There is nothing real and nothing imagined, but from distance", writes Baudrillard. "But what happens when the distance between them increases?"[45]

Back to the question of whether testimony is a simulacrum. Testimony is an event in and of itself that presents and revives an experience that occurred but does not intend and does not convey the pure version of the event.

As Sartre writes in his book "*Nausea*" (1938):

> I can search the past in vain, I can only find these scraps of images and I am not sure what they represent, whether they are memories or just fiction.[46]

Testimony remains a subjective description of the event that happened. It is not the reality that was, but it is the thing closest to it. It does not harm the nature of the event and does not become a 'sovereign' over the occurrence. It is a reflection of the actuality, represents it and maintains a direct connection between it and the real event. There is nothing in the testimony of what Baudrillard characterizes simulacra such as "A clearance sale of truth."[47]

In this context, it is appropriate to refer to the work of Claude Lanzman as the Director of the film "Shoah", in which testimony is a weighty subject. Lanzmann struggled with the impossibility of representing the Shoah and insisted on the need to find approaches that transcend the representation of testimony itself, as he notes: "It is always necessary to think of how not to represent in order to testify."[48]

List of References and Notes

1 Berkeley, George (1710): *A Treatise Concerning the Principles of Human Knowledge* "But, say you, surely there is nothing easier than for me to imagine trees, for instance, in a park . . . and nobody by to perceive them. . . . The objects of sense exist only when they are perceived; the trees therefore are in the garden . . . no longer than while there is somebody by to perceive them."

2 Austin, John Langshaw (1961): *Philosophical Papers*, ed. J. O. Urmson and G. J. Warnock. Oxford University Press, Oxford (1979).

3 Coady, Cecil Anthony John (1992): *Testimony: A Philosophical Study*. Clarendon Press, Oxford. Gives an example of two common information sentences. One: A man tells his friend that no mail has been received for him today; two: that his secretary said he did not receive mail that day. Both constitute an illocutionary expression; we were an expression in which the action is done in the utterance of the expression.

4 Felman, Shoshna and Laub, Dori (1992): *Crisis of Witnessing in Literature, Psychoanalysis, and History*. Routledge, Great Britan; Taylor and Francis, New York.

5 Ibid., p. 5.

6 Ibid., pp. 206–207.

7 Ibid., p. 5.

8 Sagi, Avi (2009): *The Human Voyage to Meaning*. Bar Ilan University Press, Ramat Gan, Israel, p. 157. Hebrew.

9 The etymology of 'testimony' and 'witnessing' unites them to one phenomenon. In Old English – *witnes* (with one S), means both testimony and witnessing, that is to say – Bearing witness means also testifying. In Hebrew there is one word for both acts, the word: '*edut*', originated in the Bible, means giving testimony and bearing witness.

10 For example, witnesses at a wedding ceremony are not involved yet without them the ceremony would not be valid.

11 Baldwin, Thomas (1962): *Merleau-Ponty, Maurice: Basic Writings*. Taylor and Francis, New York, NY (Kindle Locations 5873–5876).

12 Buber, Martin (1923): *I and Thou*. Translated into English (1937). Scribner Classics Martino Publishing, Eastford, CT, p. 158.

13 Sagi, Avi (2012): *Facing Others and Otherness: The Ethics of Inner Retreat*. Hakibbutz Hameuchad Publishing House, Bnei Brak, Israel, pp. 88–106. Hebrew.

14 Ibid., pp. 11–12.

15 Foucault, Michel (2018): *Spaces of Crisis and Critique: Heterotopias beyond Foucault*. Bloomsbury Academic, Oxford, New York, Sydney and New Delhi.

16 Sagi, Avi (2009): *The Human Voyage to Meaning*. Bar Ilan University Press, Ramat Gan, Israel, p. 48. Hebrew.

17 Ibid., p. 43.

18 De Saussure, Ferdinand (1916): *Course in General Linguistic*, Translation from French: Avner Lahav, Reslling, Tel-Aviv, Israel (2005) p. 131.

19 Sagi (2009), pp. 31, 43.

20 Ibid., p. 40.

21 In German a witness is termed '*der zeuge*' which means 'eyewitness'.

22 Felman, Shoshana and Laub, Dori (1992): *Testimony: Crises of Witnessing in Literature, Psychoanalysis and History*. Routledge, Great Britain; Taylor and Francis, New York (1992).
    Ibid., p. 101.

23 Midrash Tanchuma, Parashat Noach 25, presented in a complete Torah (Genesis 11:40).

24 Rashi.

25 There are cases of testimony in which sight and observation do not play any role. For example, when a person testifies about an experience of his past, or about a secret that is created within him, or about his physical or mental state. Moreover, even academic evidence, like a review of mathematical formulas or revelations about the state of the planet, are obtained without being able to observe them.

26 Wittgenstein, Ludvig (1953): *Philosophical Investigations*. Blackwell Publishing, London, England, # 80.

27 Wittgenstein, Ludvig (1967): *Lectures and Conversations on Aesthetics and Psychology*. Imprint Blackwell Publishing, London, England, # 197:1.

28 Ibid., # 143.

29 Heidegger, Martin (1935): *The Origin of the Act of Art*. Harper Collins, New York, NY, p. 188.

30 Ibid., p. 188.

31 Bakhtin, M. Michael (1986): *Speech Genres and Other Late Essays*. University of Texas Press, Austin, TX, p. 371.

32 Sovran, Tamar (2006): *Language and Meaning: The Birth and Growth of Cognitive Semantics*. University of Haifa Press, Haifa, Israel, pp. 2–3. Hebrew.

33 Sagi (2009), p. 39.

34 Ibid.

35 Barthes, Ronald (1967): *Elements of Semiology*. Hilland and Wang, New York, NY.

36 Heidegger, Martin (1927): "Letter on Humanism". In Martin Heidegger, *Basic Writings*, trans. David Farrell Krell. Routledge & Kegan Paul, London (1978).

37 Ibid., p. 5.

38 Ibid., p. 115.

39 Heidegger, Martin (1978): *Heidegger and Modern Philosophy: Critical Essays*. Yale University Press, New Haven, pp. 189–242.

40 Imagination plays a significant part in bringing an experience from the past into the present, but this is not the place to deal with that subject.

41 A Shakespearian monologue has a significant effect on those present, whether it is their experience or their being. "All the world is a stage" . . . for example is a monologue that affects me every time I read or hear it. What I intend to say here is not related to a lecture or a theatrical play but rather a conversation between two or more in which the speaker wants to express his opinion without having any interest in the views of others and without waiting for them to respond.

42 Rosenzweig, Franz, who started his philosophical work at the beginning of the 20th century Particularly in his book: Between the Rivers: Selected Essays and – The booklet: Understanding the Sick and the Healthy Psych: A View of World, Man, and God (1921) – on the importance of dialogic speech in a person's experience of existence.

43 Amir, Yehoyada (2008): *Towards a Renewal of Franz Rosenzweig's Philosophical Direction on the Subject of the Healthy Psyche.* Resling, Tel-Aviv, Israel, pp. 7–32.

44 Baudrillard, Jean (1981): *Simulacra and Simulation the Body, in Theory: Histories of Cultural Materialism.* "The French", Hakibutz Hameuchad Publishing House Ltd, Bnei Brak, Israel (2007) (Hebrew).

45 Ibid.

46 Sartre, Jean-Paul (1938): *Nausea.* New Directions Paperback, New York City, NY (1981), p. 63.

47 Sartre (1981), pp. 12–13.

48 Lanzmann, Claud, In an interview given to a private web site following his final film *The Last of the Unjust* (2013).

Chapter 2

A Paradigmatic Turning Point in the Understanding of the Concept of Testimony

Zipi Rosenberg Schipper

Introduction

The meaning of the concept of spoken testimony has changed over time, both epistemologically and in terms of the value attached to it, a rare phenomenon in the narrative of concepts. Towards the 1990s, views began to be expressed in philosophical literature, pointing to the injustice of the lack of academic recognition accorded to testimony. Felman and Laub (1992) wrote: "The academic approach to testimony lacks the dimension of philosophical, literary and human depth which it warrants".[1]

Dominick LaCapra (2001) argued that: "Although the phenomenon of testimony is widespread and known . . . up till now, there has been very little, if any, research . . . so as to gain an understanding of the very essence of the phenomenon."[2]

The process of change in the perception of the concept of spoken testimony was not a conscious historical recognition, nor was it the outcome of a guiding hand. Very few researchers and historians related to it. Prominent among those who did, are Coady (1992), Felman and Laub (1992) and Dominick LaCapra (2001).

But even they, although writing about the influence of testimony or the lack of it, mainly referred to the content that passes through it and not to the act of testimony itself.

The Background to the Turning Point

Spoken testimony was perceived as a tool intended to complete, validate and shed light on an unclear reality. A blood-soaked history, and the development of psychoanalysis, raised the general awareness of psychic trauma of nations and individuals and redefined the meaning of testimony and its importance in the context of loss and death.

The paradigmatic turn in the meaning of the concept and the significant change of its "image of knowledge"[3] occurred towards the last decade of the 20th century. Even though its roots were established in the first half of the century, it only crystallized fifty years later.

DOI: 10.4324/9781003403920-3

The attitude to spoken testimony changed in a 'natural' way, and there was almost no philosophical or psychological preoccupation justifying or resisting its new ethical or moral value.

The Eichmann Trial and the Film "Shoah" as Landmarks in the Discourse on Testimony

There is a kind of consensus among researchers and historians that the "Eichman trial" held in Israel (1961–1962), which was broadcast in real-time throughout the world, was a watershed in the discourse on testimony. However, an examination of the events after the trial reveals that in regard to the status of testimony, the turn did not happen then, but only thirty years later, when society and, in its footsteps, the analysts were more prepared to accept conceptual changes.

The 1960s were a period of skepticism during which people clung to what existed. The trial did indeed strongly highlight the value of the concept of testimony, and the controversial decision to call Holocaust survivors[4] to the witness stand to identify Eichmann proved to be successful both legally and historically.

Following the trial, the "knot of silence",[5] which until then was the sad fate of the Holocaust survivors, was broken, and their social status in Israel and around the world has indeed changed significantly. But a close examination of social or political developments in the years after shows that its influence on the standing of the discourse of testimony remained limited.

As a rule, a change in the image of knowledge of a concept occurs when there is a shift in philosophical views.[6] This, indeed, is a necessary but insufficient condition. The philosophical or historical dynamic of changes in the image of a concept shows that although changes in its image of knowledge gain recognition with the development of a fitting philosophy, their roots are deeper and, generally, are structured on social characteristics.[7] That's what happened here, the recognition of the turn in the understanding of the concept of spoken testimony occurred much after the events that led to it had already taken place.

In the years following World War II, the Western world was preoccupied with the rehabilitation of the destruction, and the "philosophical silence" prevailed.[8] Positivism, the spirit of enlightenment and modernism, still governed the philosophical, psychological and cultural-societal arena, And so, a dramatic event such as the Eichman trial, which from historical and social perspective, was of huge importance, in relation to the question of testimony, did not lead to a shift in the status of the testimonial discourse.

Changes in 'Forms' of Discourse

In his book "*The Archaeology of Knowledge*" (1969), Michel Foucault sought to follow the historical changes in "forms of discourse".[9] According to Foucault, forms of discourse change in line with the historical context and their influence is determined by the philosophical and social setting in which they occur. In Foucault's view, the 'event' and the historical context inspire one another.

Foucault's attention turned to the breach and rifts in historical processes, which in his words, are "the points of the discourse's rupture".[10] At such a point in time, another possibility could be created, and a transition of discourse from the hegemony of one discipline to the hegemony of another discipline takes place.

In the course of history, there are events that constitute such a point, and they are not necessarily particularly significant from a historical point of view. The fact that they are related to a fitting historical ideology increases their influence.

Foucault asserts that due to a deepening of our understanding of distinct events, we learn about historical processes. That is, the 'breaking point of a discourse' is a combination of a general ideological rupture with a single significant event linked to that ideological breach. One such event was Claude Lanzman's film, "Shoah" (1985).

The Historical Context

During the last third of the 20th century, the Western world was deprived of its previously predominant systems of thought in virtually every field. Descartes's epistemological dominance was weakened, and, in parallel, there was evident disappointment in science as a comprehensive solution to life's questions.

A new stream of thought that had developed filled the lacuna – postmodernism along with the 'deconstruction' stream of thought, which was one of its pillars. These encouraged critical thinking in order to pinpoint and deconstruct concepts regarded as axiomatic. Thus, philosophical conventions were 'broken'. Acceptable social phenomena were formulated in a different way.

No less dominant in changing worldviews was the strengthening of the feminist movement. Feminist epistemology, which essentially presented an anti-Cartesian stance, encouraged dialectics and reciprocity and expressed opposition to dichotomies and dualism, such as between object and subject, soma and consciousness, or between emotion and thought. Following that, the position of the 'other' rose, as did the status of social dialogues or situations of mutuality, of contexts and perspectives (Orange 2010).

All of these were highly relevant to the strengthening of the status of testimony, and indeed the discourse on testimony moved from the margins to the forefront of the cultural-social debate.

From a Cinematic to a Formative Event

It was in this philosophical, intellectual atmosphere that Claude Lanzmann's film, "Shoah" – comprised entirely of testimonies – was released (1985). Lanzmann refused to use archival material, incorporate a plot to the film or add narration linked to images. He contended that all of these distort the context and that only personal testimony could be considered to be the authentic voice of the horrific events that were there. Lantzman used first-hand evidence from people who had been there and spent eleven years editing these testimonies himself.

Lanzmann does not offer viewers cathartic moments. He does not talk about the continuity of life and does not try to pacify. He focuses on the place of personal testimony in an individual's life. In Lanzmann's view, the question: 'How do you live with the trauma?' is inadequate because it is there all the time, like a subtext of the spoken testimony.

In an interview after the screening of the film, Lanzmann explained that the structure of a film must determine its own intelligibility: He claims: "I knew very early on that I would not use the archives."[11] Later in this interview, he 'identifies' with Sartre's thinking, in the sense that a person is never a character in his life, but only in the story of his life; in his words:

> Film is not made up of memories . . . The film annuls the distance between the past and the present and only by turning the witnesses into "images" and "actors" can one bring the past into the present.

A notable feature of the film is the multiplicity of languages. The spoken testimonies in it are asked, responded to, repeated and responded to in French, German, English, Yiddish, Hebrew, Sicilian and Polish. Thus, Lanzmann doubles and triples the content of the evidence.

Felman and Laub (1992) refer to this technique:

> The multiplicity of languages . . . necessitates the presence of a professional translator[12] as an intermediary between the witnesses and Lanzmann who was their interviewer. "The task of the translator" (according to Walter Benjamin),[13] is carried out within the film, not merely by the professional interpreter, but also by the two actors – the historian: Raul Hilberg, and the filmmaker: Claude Lanzmann, the historian is, thus, in the film, neither the last word of knowledge nor the ultimate authority on history, but rather, one more topographical and cognitive position of *yet another witness*
>
> (Italics in the original.)[14]

Another point of crucial importance rooted in the essence of cinema is the intermingling of the two senses – sight and hearing. This combination accentuates the difference between the Eichmann trial and the film "Shoah" and expresses something fundamental about the action of the testimony itself, namely the complexity of conveying a message of a moving event or a powerful experience to a listener who cannot experience with his own senses what was said in the testimony.

The Eichmann trial, in contrast to the film "Shoah", spoke only of a past and left a permanent set of dichotomies between then and now, there and here and them and us. The film "Shoah", on the other hand, addresses the present, both the people in the present, in whom the past documented in the film is embedded, and also those who live in its shadow – which is all of us.

At the Eichmann trial, the witnesses were heard but not seen. Throughout the trial, the voices of the survivors transfixed the public. This was especially true of the Jewish public, but not only. Although there were scenes from the trial that were filmed, they were not shown to a wide audience.

Moreover, even later, in Haim Guri's dramatic film "The 81st Blow" (1974), which spoke of the witness being beaten 80 times and remaining alive, the line that placed the witnesses as 'heard but not seen' continued. This emphasized the absence rather than the presence of the witnesses' images.

Lantzman's special strategy of using the cinematic medium, fully and professionally, which mingles watching the speakers and hearing their voices, repeating the same testimony in a multiplicity of languages, had the effect of engaging the viewer's entire being and senses until the testimonies became etched in the viewer's mind and didn't let go of him.

The advantage of the cinema to integrate messages in our consciousness has been dramatically proven. The tension between the position that the 'Shoah' is unrepresentable and the urge of personal and social drive, or order to tell it, finds its way into the art of cinema and is a lesson of the cinematic medium's capacity to say what cannot be said in any other way:

As Lanzman puts it:

> Truth needs the art of cinema to convey it to viewers, so that it is illustrated in our consciousness, as witnesses.[15]

That the film was a formative event in the discourse of testimony is evident from what followed its release. About a year after its first public showing, the Amcha Organization was established in Israel in 1987.[16] Six years later, the International Institute for Holocaust Studies (1993) was established at Yad Vashem in Jerusalem, at the same time as Steven Spielberg's film, "Schindler's List", was first screened. In 1994, The Testimonies Project was launched in the United States, and a year later, the Shoah Museum was opened in Washington. More and more such commemorations were to follow.

The Turning Point and Its Impact

During centuries of philosophical thought, the approach to spoken testimony was viewed as a concept whose entire value was linked to its outcome. Its altered image occurred only after testimony was recognized as an action whose purpose lay in its delivery. It thus became what can be termed 'pure testimony', and only then, its healing qualities were also discovered.

In the wake of the turning point, the boundaries of the discourse on testimony were breached, the publication of survivors' testimonies increased and researchers from various disciplines started to express their views on additional aspects of testimony beyond the epistemological. The emphasis moved to aspects related to the emotional experience of the witness delivering his testimony and the experience of the recipient. This interest led to the recognition that testimony, willingly given and in and of itself, is much more than a description of a certain state of affairs. Such testimony carries a powerful experiential and emotional significance, both for the witnessing narrator and the listener.

The lack of purpose in external action leads the listener to move his emotional gaze off his own volition and needs and turn that gaze to view the other. Whilst the testimony is being delivered, there is nothing for him to do other than to experience the testimony being heard by him.

Following the acknowledgment of testimony as an alleviator of distress, it gained recognition in social culture and art; its status in the therapeutic narrative rose and, ironically, also grew in the field of epistemology.

A dramatic example of the social impact of the multiplicity of testimonies can be seen in the profound change that took place in the personal and social status of 'Shoah' survivors, who had emigrated to Israel, a change that happened only when the 'thunder' of their spoken testimonies began to be heard.

As said, the immigrants were perceived as a 'different' group and, in many ways, even inferior to it. Listening to the numerous personal testimonies led to the mutual sense of 'foreignness' increasingly diminishing, the mutual involvement growing and their enormous contribution in all fields of knowledge and culture or art getting recognized. Prominent expressions of this are evident in local literature, poetry, social culture, schools, youth movements and universities.

The semantic field of the concept of testimony changed, and with it, both the images, as well as the questions that were being asked. When the dominant aspect of testimony was that of a medium that supplied information, its semantic field included concepts such as trust, doubt, epistemology, information, proof, statement, fact, truth and memory.

The semantic field of testimony as a medium of healing, on the other hand, includes psychological terms such as trust, validation, recognition, developmental need, sharing, alleviation of distress, reciprocity, contribution to self-establishment and supporting recovery.

Trust is the only common keyword.

This development transferred the phenomenon of testimony, which had been wholly in the epistemological space of the 'question of certainty', to the space that developed between it and the 'question of the other'. This marked the philosophical place of the phenomenon of spoken testimony in intermediate spaces – between objectivity and subjectivity, between subjects, between inner and outer reality, between past and present, between history and story and between patient and therapist.

Dominik La Capra (2001; 2014) writes on the turning point in the concept of testimony:

> The interest in testimonies has been on the rise in the course of the last twenty years or so . . . one important role for testimonies is to serve as a supplement to more standard documentary sources in history. But they may at times be of

limited value when used narrowly to derive facts about events in the past. Historians who see testimonies as sources of facts or information about the past are justifiably concerned about their reliability. Less justifiably, they are at times prone to dismiss an interest in them. The importance of testimonies becomes more apparent when they are related to the way they provide something other than purely documentary knowledge.[17]

As an illustration – LaCapra cites Dori Laub in his book *"Testimony"*, written together with Shoshana Felman:

A woman in her late sixties was narrating her Auschwitz experience to interviewers from the Video Archive for Holocaust Testimonies and says, "All of a sudden," she said, "we saw four chimneys going up in flames, exploding . . ." Many months later, a conference of historians, psychoanalysts, and artists, gathered to reflect on the relation of education to the Holocaust, watched the videotaped testimony of the woman . . . "The testimony was not accurate", historians claimed. The number of chimneys was misrepresented. Historically, only one chimney was blown up, not all four. Since the memory of the testifying woman turned out to be, in this way, fallible, one could not accept, nor give credence to her whole account of the events.

The psychoanalyst who had been one of the interviewers of this woman, profoundly disagreed. "The woman was testifying," he insisted, "not to the number of the chimneys blown up, but to something else, more radical, more crucial: the reality of an unimaginable occurrence. The number mattered less than the fact of the occurrence. The event itself was almost inconceivable. The woman testified to an event that broke the all-compelling frame of Auschwitz, where Jewish armed revolts just did not happen, and had no place. She testified to the breakage of a framework. That was historical truth."[18]

At a certain intense point in her narrative, as Laub puts it, "**she was there!**"[19]

The Listening Experience

In spoken testimony, there is sometimes a struggle with pieces of memory or with fragments of images and dreams, and all this in an attempt to reassume control over his life. In such cases, it is essential that there be an attentive witness who will create an atmosphere of trust, security and 'being at home'.

Felman and Laub (1992) write:

Testimonies are not Monologues. They cannot take place in solitude . . . For the testimonial process to take place, there needs to be a bonding, the intimate and total presence of an-other – in the position of one who hears . . . The task of the listener is to be unobtrusively present, throughout the testimony; even when and if at moments the narrator becomes absent, reaches an almost detached state. The listener has to respond very subtly to cues the narrator is giving that s/he wants to come back, to resume contact . . . there has to be an abundance of holding and of emotional investment in the encounter, to keep alive the witnessing narration; otherwise, the whole experience of the testimony can end up in silence, in complete withholding.[20]

Against the difficulty of recounting, there is the great strain of listening.

Jorje Semprún, in his book "*Literature or Life*" (1994), writes about the difficulty of listening to traumatic testimony:

He spoke for a long while; we listened to him in silence, frozen in the pallid anguish of his story. Suddenly . . . we realized that wintry night had fallen . . . We had sunk body and soul, into the night of that story, suffocating, without any sense of time.[21]

There is here a complex duality. On the one hand, the recipient must be imperceptible, whilst on the other hand, be listening in an active presence. The meaning of attention in spoken testimony is no less than to constitute the existence of testimony. The recipient who "signs the testimony"[22] is liable to endure an uneasy passage which may be expressed in physical and mental responses.

Felman and Laub (1992) point out some of the ways in which the recipient tries to cope with or defend himself against the testimony since he cannot distance himself from listening to it nor can it be mediated: Common responses include paralysis of hearing brought about by a fear of being engulfed and feelings of anger and rage which are unconsciously directed at the testimony's narrator.[23]

It is important to remember that not every testimony is about trauma and that, as already noted, one of the main objectives of this book is to unfasten the binding connection between testimony and trauma. Also, there are occasions when there isn't a need for such a great level of emotional support, but there is always a requirement for being present, for trust and attention.

List of References and Notes

1 Felman, Shoshana and Laub, Dori (1992): *Testimony: Crises of Witnessing in Literature, Psychoanalysis and History*. Routledge, Great Britain; Taylor and Francis, New York.

2 LaCapra, Dominick (2001): *Writing History, Writing Trauma*. Johns Hopkins University Press, Baltimore, MD (2014).

3 The phrase "image of knowledge" was coined by Elkana (Elkana 1981). According to him, at any given time, images of state of knowledge develop in society that relate to methods, open problems, theoretical networks and even deeply to the metaphysics of science. These images of knowledge determine perspectives on knowledge (views of knowledge in the world). These are beliefs that develop socially and relate to the role of science (understanding, foresight), the nature of truth (certainty, reasonableness) and sources of knowledge (rational considerations or through the senses) and create images of scientific concepts that are time-dependent and culture-dependent. It is in the power

of these images of knowledge to determine what will be considered important, interesting, challenging, absurd or dangerous. This field of knowledge does not formulate a list of legitimate sources for the development of perspectives. It is a space of images that moves and depends on time, place, culture or discipline (Ibid., pp. 76–71); it seems clear that the change in the image of the knowledge of the concept of testimony is such a case.

4   Hannah Arendt's opposition to the use of survivors as prosecution witnesses in a court of law is well known. Her view was expressed in a series of articles on the trial published in the magazine 'The New Yorker' and especially in her book *The Eichman Trial: The Banality of Evi* (1963).

5   Ben Naftali, Berkowitz, Michal (1993): "The Israeli Philosophers and the Shoah". In: *Theory and Criticism*. The Van Leer Jerusalem Institute, Jerusalem, Hakibbutz Hameuhad, Bnei Brak Israel, Vol. 4, pp. 57–78.

6   Govrin, Aner (2006): "The Dilemma of Contemporary Psychoanalysis: Toward a 'Knowing' Post-Postmodernism". *Journal of the American Psychoanalytic Association*, 54 (2), pp. 510–511.

7   Elkana, Yehuda (1981): "A Programmatic Attempt at an Anthropology of Science". In: *Sciences and Cultures* (ed. E. Mendelson & Y. Elkana), Reidel, Dordrecht (1998), pp. 1–76.

8   Ben Naftali (1993), p. 57.

9   Foucault, Paul Michel (1969): *The Archaeology of Knowledge & the Discourse on Language*. Editions Gallimard, Tavistock Publications Limited, London (1972).

10 Ibid., p. 74.

11 From an interview given by Lanzmann immediately after the screening of the film "Shoah" to correspondents from "Yad Vashem".

12 Felman, Shoshana and Laub, Dori (1992): *Crises of Witnessing in Literature, Psychoanalysis and History*. Routledge, Great Britan; Taylor and Francis, New York, p. 211.

13 Benjamin, Walter (1923): "The Task of the Translator". In: Walter Benjamin, *Illuminations: Essays and Reflections*. Mariner Books Houghton Mifflin Harcourt, Boston and New York (2019).

14 Felman and Laub (1992), p. 213.

15 Claud Lanzman, in an interview with Deborah Jerome, "The Man behind Shoah" 25.10.1985.

16 The Israeli Center for Psychological and Social Support, for Holocaust Survivors and the Second Generation.

17 LaCapra, Dominick (2001): *Writing History, Writing Trauma* (Parallax: Re-Visions of Culture and Society). Johns Hopkins University Press, Baltimore, MD (2014).

18 Felman and Laub (1992), p. 60.

19 Ibid., pp. 70–77.

20 Ibid., pp. 70–71.

21 Semprún, Jorje (1994): *Literature or Life*. Penguin Books, London and New York, pp. 50–51.

22 Felman and Laub (1992), pp. 70–71.

23 Ibid.

Chapter 3

Aspects and Images of Personal Testimony

Zipi Rosenberg Schipper

Introduction

Spoken testimony is an extensive and complex phenomenon, and any given definition will not sum it up. In order to obtain a more comprehensive picture in what follows, a wide fan of aspects and images and portrayal of various angles of personal testimony – taken from the world of prose and poetry, as well as from the fields of philosophy, psychology and literary research – will be described.

Testimony as an Ethical and Moral Act

The moral aspect of testimony involves the relationship between a person and the other and between a person and himself. It has already been discussed in Halakhic tradition and was mainly expressed by the principle of the duty to testify. The idea behind this aspect is linked to social solidarity, to the good of society and the good of the individual. This personal and social aspect still exists today and is very strongly evident in Shoah research.

Wiesel (1984) refers to this duty: "As a Holocaust survivor, my role is the role of the witness . . . not to tell or to tell another story, is to commit perjury".[1]

Primo Levi adds to that:

> the Lagers were a political phenomenon, and because the politicians – to a far greater extent than the Jews and the common criminals (the three main categories of prisoners, as we know) – were equipped with an educational background that enabled them to interpret the events they witnessed . . . they realized that bearing witness was an act of war against fascism.[2]

Felman and Laub (1992) relate to these sayings and expand on the ethical aspect of testimony:

> To testify – to vow to tell, to promise and produce one's own speech as material evidence for truth – is to accomplish a speech act.[3]

DOI: 10.4324/9781003403920-4

And in another place:

> To take responsibility in the act of speaking about the history, or the kernel of truth of event, for its validity, and its applications, goes beyond the personal towards the general.[4]

Testimony as a Means of Relief

"Testimony is first and foremost a means of relief."[5]

"First Person Essays", **Appelfeld, Aharon (1979)**

Paul Celan speaks on the loneliness of a witness who carries a testimony that is unique to him. According to Celan, to bear witness is to bear the solitude of a responsibility, and to bear the responsibility, precisely, of that solitude. Felman and Laub (1992) relate to this notion and say that in a paradoxical way: "Dew to the fact that testimony is addressed to others it breaks the boundaries of this solitude position".[6]

Testimony does indeed come from the depths of a person's inner loneliness. But the moment of its delivery and its coming to light, in front of a listening witness, is the antithesis of solitude. More than that, the main theme of spoken testimony is the communion and sharing of an emotional burden, the non-sharing of which is oppressive to the person and can harm him. By all accounts, testimony given by choice before an attentive recipient alleviates loneliness.

This notion is reinforced by many writers and poets; here is one of them, an excerpt from a poem by Samuel Taylor Coleridge (1798):

"The Rime of the Ancient Mariner"
Since then, at an uncertain hour,
That agony returns:
And till my ghastly tale is told,
This heart within me burns.[7]

And more about the aspect of relief in the discussion of the objective of testimony.

Testimony as a Transitional Space

A thing that appears in front of the senses and is processed by the subject (like witnessing) is a "phenomenon that embodies an encounter between the inner and the external and between subject and object"[8] (Eran Dorfman, in the introduction to "The Look" by Jean Paul Sartre).

Every attempt to conceptualize the act of testimony ends with locating it within intermediate or transitional spaces.

The Diversity of Transitional Spaces in the Process of Testimony

- Transition between times. Between events in the past and the story in the present.
- Transition between object and subject or between subjects.
- Transition between the inner and the external reality.
- Transition between the world of inner silenced experience to the stream of sound and words.
- Transition between a latent and private experience and an interpersonal space.
- And an intermediate space between opposing worldviews, as in the psychoanalytic field.[9]

Transitional space is an 'in-between space', and in this sense, it can also be seen as a 'liminal state', which is a fundamentally unstable situation, to some extent fragile, but at the same time constitutes a place of creation and formation.[10]

From Turner's (1989) studies of the rites of passage using the model developed by Arnold van Gennep (1909),[11] we learn that this transition is not a linear boundary but a space, especially a space of time. According to Turner, a liminal state is presented to us as "a moment in and out of time."[12] Testimony is indeed "a moment within and outside of time".

Testimony as a 'Voyage Between Times'

In their book "*Testimony*", Felman and Laub (1992) describe spoken testimony as a story that connects narrative and history. The meaning of this image is not only aimed at the space that connects experience and time but also reflects the dynamics of the change of the experience within this space, which takes place within the narrator's 'psyche'.

Walter Benjamin commented on this:

> The story as speech, is one of the oldest forms of conveying information. It does not intend to convey the pure version 'per se' of the event (as is done by the testimony that conveys technical knowledge) but the story immerses the event in the life of the narrator, so that it is conveyed to his listeners as a personal experience.
>
> (Parenthesis in the original.)[13]

Yehuda Amichai, the poet, saw the act of spoken testimony as "*A Voyage of the Soul*".[14] In this 'voyage', he differentiated between two kinds of time: "The time that revolves and returns, and the time that flows and goes" (from the poems stored in Amichai's estate).

The story of testimony does indeed move between past and present. Yet, the time line of the story's movement is quite the opposite. The occurrence of the event and the story about it take place in reverse direction. The testimony's story starts at the end, a significant fact in the design of the story.[15]

On the concept of testimony as a story of a journey between personal times, Sartre writes his book "Nausea" (1938):

> I build memories with my present self. I am cast out, forsaken in the present. I vainly try to rejoin the past, I cannot escape . . . If I were ever to go on a trip, I think I should make written notes of the slightest traits of my character before leaving, so that when I return, I would be able to compare what I was and what I had become . . . But the end is there, transforming everything . . . And the story goes on in the reverse: instants have stopped piling themselves in a lighthearted way one on top of the other, they are snapped up by the end of the story which draws them and each one of them in turn, draws out the preceding instant.[16]

Motif of Survival in Spoken Testimony

"To speak yourself is to survive"

"The Book of Disquiet", **Pessoa, Fernando** (2002)

Listening to spoken testimony touches upon the life instinct, and the clearest expression of this is developmental. The normal development of a child depends on the trust he feels towards what the adults in his near surroundings, such as parents or teachers, say and towards listening to them.

In his *"The Book of Disquiet"* (2001–2002 & 2017), Pessoa relates to the power of the verbal statement in human life. According to him, a literal description of something benefits the speaker, improves the thing itself and beautifies it. Spoken testimony, in his view, gives life to the spoken matter.

Below are some of Pessoa's thoughts on spoken testimony in the book:

- "I enjoy speaking. Or rather, I enjoy wording. Words for me are tangible bodies."[17]
- "To say is to renew . . ."[18]
- "To express something is to conserve its virtue".[19]
- "To express something is to conserve its virtue and remove its terror".
- "Fields are greener in their description than in their actual greenness. Flowers, if described with phrases that define them in the air of the imagination, will have colours with a durability not found in cellular life".[20]

Commenting on Pessoa's thoughts Avi Sagi (2009) notes:

> Pessoa, like Kierkegaard before him, experienced the tension between existence and consciousness . . . on the one hand existence is not embodied in spoken testimony, yet on the other hand, it is an individual's only way to find meaning in what he has experienced.[21]

Testimony as a Bridge

In my view, the most fitting metaphor for spoken personal testimony is a bridge. As said, testimony exists in intermediate spaces and is a kind of link between areas, such as: between narrative and history, between subject and object, between past and present, between inside and outside and between an inner experience and inter-personal space. A bridge, by its very nature, connects two banks and allows movement between them, similar to the testimony being delivered.

Felman and Laub agree. According to them: "the narrator-as-eyewitness is a testimonial bridge."[22]

Avi Sagi as well, relates to this – "Spoken testimony is the mechanism of processing, interpreting and judging, that bridges between times."[23]

Immanent Elements in the Act of Testimony

The Component of Interpretation in Testimony

"By his nature, a person is an interpreting entity",[24] meaning that interpretation is an inherent part of listening, for in every listening, there are immediately certain determinations as to the voice of the speaker or the location of the speech.

Assuming that the existence of a testimony is conditioned on the listening of a recipient, it can be said that interpretation is an inherent element of testimony. Thus, any testimony delivered is not free from interpretation of both the addressor and the addressee.

Primo Levi refers to this: "Prosecutors are quite familiar with this phenomenon: two eyewitnesses to the same deed, almost never describe it in the same way and in the same words."[25]

Walter Benjamin (1996), who thought a lot about transcription and originality, thought highly of spoken testimonies, noting that the story is never an accurate description of what was happening but an experiential description with a personal and subjective interpretation, and it is good that it is so.[26]

Sartre (1932 [1978]) also refers to the interpretive element in the story of testimony, and again in "Nausea":

> Nothing happens while you live. The scenery changes, people come in and go out, that's all. There are no beginnings. Days are tacked on to days without rhyme or reason. . . . That's living. But everything changes when you tell about your life; it's a change no one notices. The proof is that people talk about true stories. As if there could possibly be true stories; things happen one way, and we tell about them in the opposite sense. You seem to start at the beginning.[27]

Testimony as a Reflective Process and the Element of 'Return'

Testimony's story, as a piece of life, is a reflective course through which a person sees what had happened to him.

Sagi (2009) writes about the reflective moment in the story of testimony:

> An occurrence is something that a person experiences, but is not always aware of its meaning, or its context . . . The central function of the testimony is not in seeing the reality, but reshaping it.[28]

One Aspect of 'Return'

Spoken testimony is an expression in words of an inner experience of a real occurrence. In this, testimony is a kind of repetition (return) of the event.

Milan Kundera expresses this notion in his book "*The Unbearable Lightness of Being*" (1984) by the saying: "*Einmal ist keinmal*" ("**once is never**").

Kundera emphasizes the element of 'repetition' present in testimony and attributes to it a moral advantage. The repetition, in his view, adds to the gravity of the event, the gravity of being.

Kundera notes:

> The idea of eternal return implies a perspective from which things appear other than as we know them: they appear without the mitigating circumstance of their transitory nature. This mitigating circumstance prevents us from coming to a verdict. For how we condemn something that is ephemeral, in transit? In the sunset of dissolution, everything is illuminated by the aura of nostalgia, even the guillotine . . . This reconciliation with Hitler reveals the profound moral perversity of a world that rests essentially on the non-existence of return, for in this world everything is pardoned in advance and therefore everything cynically permitted . . . Whilst in the world of eternal return the weight of unbearable responsibility, lies heavily on every move we make. This is why Nietzsche called the idea of eternal return the heaviest of burdens.
>
> (*das schwerste Gewicht*)[29]

Poets and writers often wrote about the one-off in our life, or the non-return, and the enormous implications of that.

Among them is Yehuda Amichai:

> "I am a prophet of what was"
> *Life, I think, is a series of rehearsals*
> *for the real show. In a rehearsal you can still*
> *make changes, . . . – up until the real show.*
> *Then there is no changing. And it makes no difference*
> *The show closes right after opening night.*[30]
> **Yehuda Amichai, *Open, Closed, Open* (2000)**

A Different Aspect of 'Return'

The reflective aspect of a story of testimony is not directed at a return to the past but to a deviation 'out of the self' and a movement of return to it inwardly. It connects to Kierkegaard's 'element of return', which says that, in fact, a story of testimony relating to a person's life enables him to deviate from himself and return to himself. The Kierkegaardian solution sought to find a complex way to preserve the tense relationship between life and its story.

In a life story, there is an exit outside that is infinite and a return to real life that is finite. This return works on the 'I'. The main function of the 'return movement' is to shape the self.

According to Sartre (1932), the person in his life is not a character, only in the story about his life, in which he is: "the protagonist of the story"[31] since the character of the person in the story deviates from his own self.

Sagi (2009) related to this

> In every act of storytelling, the ego undergoes a process of objectification, which for a moment takes from the self its real life and transforms it into an object. However, this moment does not replace existence itself. It is only a moment. The various stories are different possibilities of existence . . . The story can "free" the person from his forced real existence . . . and it can be a critical moment through which a person will re-examine his attitude to his actual existence.[32]

What better way is there to end this paragraph on the moment of return in the phenomenon of testimony than with the words of longing and yearning for the return of 'undeciphered testimony', which is beautifully described by Marcel Proust in his book *"In Search of Lost Time"* (1913) and which became the best-known literary testimony of the 20th century.

Here it is:

> The tea has called up in me, but does not itself understand, and can only repeat indefinitely with a gradual loss of strength, the same testimony; which I, too, cannot interpret, though I hope at least to be able to call upon the tea for it again and to find it there presently, intact and at my disposal, for my final enlightenment.[33]

List of References and Notes

1 Felman, Shoshana and Laub, Dori (1992): *Testimony: Crises of Witnessing in Literature, Psychoanalysis and History*. Routledge, Great Britain; Taylor and Francis, New York, p. 204.
2 Levi, Primo (2015): *The Complete Works of Primo Levi*. Liveright, New York City, New York, U.S.A. ISBN 10: 0871404567, ISBN 13: 9780871404565, pp. 2416–2417.
3 Felman, Shoshana and Laub, Dori (1992): *Crises of Witnessing in Literature, Psychoanalysis and History*. Routledge, Great Britan; Taylor and Francis, New York, p. 5.
4 Ibid., p. 205.
5 Appelfeld, Aharon (1979): *Essays in the First Person*. The Zionist Library, The World Zionist Organization, Jerusalem, Israel (Hebrew).
6 Felman and Laub (1992), p. 21.
7 Coleridge, Samuel Taylor (1798): *The Rime of the Ancient Mariner*, originally published in Lyrical Ballads (1798), a collaborative venture with William Wordsworth, Start Publishing LLC (2012), distributed by Simon and Shuster, Australia.

8 Dorfman, Eran's Introduction to Jean Paul Sartre's: *The Look*, Part 3 Chapter 1 (IV) of Sartre's *Being and Nothingness*. Resling, Tel Aviv, Israel (2007) pp. 10–11 (Hebrew).

9 Wilson, Arnold (2003): "Ghosts of Paradigms Past: The Once and Future Evolution of Psychoanalytic Thought". *Journal of the American Psychoanalytic Association*, 51, pp. 825–855.

10 Turner, Victor (1969): *The Ritual Process: Structure and Anti-Structure*. Routledge, London (1996).

11 Arnold van Gennep's words (1909) in Victor Turner's book *The Ritual Process: Structure and Anti-Structure*. (1969).

12 Ibid., p. 127.

13 Benjamin, Walter (1923): "The Task of the Translator". In: Walter Benjamin, *Illuminations: "Essays and Reflections"*. Mariner Books Houghton Mifflin Harcourt, Boston, New York (2019) (p. 88 in Hebrew).

14 Amichai, Yehuda (2004): *The Fist Was Also Once an Open Hand and Fingers. Open, Close, Open*. Schocken Publishing House Ltd, Tel Aviv, Israel, p. 44 (Hebrew).

15 At this point, the discussion only expands the subject of testimony being a 'transition between times' The other transitional spaces, are discussed throughout the book.

16 Sartre, Jean-Paul (1938): *Nausea*. New Directions Paperback, New York City, NY, p. 73.

17 Pessoa, Fernando (2002): *The Book of Disquiet*. Penguin Modern Classics, Penguin Books Ltd, London, England, paragraph 259.

18 Ibid., paragraph 116.

19 Ibid., Paragraph 28.

20 Ibid.

21 Sagi, Avi (2009): *The Human Voyage to Meaning*. Bar Ilan University Press, Ramat Gan, Israel, pp. 12–13 (Hebrew).

22 Felman and Laub (1992), p. 101.

23 Sagi, Avi (2006): *The Jewish-Israeli Voyage: Culture and Identity*. Shalom Hartman Institute, Jerusalem, p. 157 (Hebrew).

24 Sagi (2009), p. 10 (Hebrew).

25 Levi (2015), p. 2420.

26 Benjamin, Walter (2000): *The Wanderer*. Hakibbutz Hameuhad Publishing House Ltd, Bnei Brak, Israel, p. 30 (Hebrew).

27 Sartre, Jean-Paul (1938): *Nausea*. New Directions Paperback, New York City, NY, p. 72.

28 Sagi (2009), p. 154 (Hebrew).

29 Kundera, Milan (1984): *The Unbearable Lightness of Being*. Faber & Faber, London, England, pp. 32–49.

30 Amichai, Yehuda (2000): *Open Closed Open* (Poem 10, HMH Books). Harcourt Inc, Publishing House, New York, NY, pp. 14–15.

31 Sartre, Jean-Paul (1936): *Nausea*. New Directions Publishing, Paperbook, New York City, NY, p. 63.

32 Sagi (2009), p. 156 (Hebrew).

33 Proust, Marcel; Classics, A to Z. *"In Search of Lost Time"* volumes. 1 to 7. ATOZ Classics. New York, NY, p. 781.

Chapter 4

Spoken Testimony, Its Epistemological Status and Its Value Standing

Zipi Rosenberg Schipper

Introduction

In a knowledge-based culture, the question of the status of spoken testimony as a good source of knowledge is a fundamental problem. "We rely on the testimonies of those around us about everything in our lives. Had we avoided information from the testimonies of others, our lives would, in a surprising way, have been poorer and weaker",[1] writes Jennifer Lackey (2009).

These issues are true in everyday life, media, academia, social sciences and humanities, as well as the exact sciences. Researchers build hypotheses based on data they have not themselves discovered. Moreover, the vast majority of research findings are confirmed and published only after colleagues have read and approved them.

Nevertheless, the academic research on testimony is flawed and partial. Even in the world of philosophy or in the therapeutic field, it is only recognized in a reflective way or when the spotlight is placed upon it.

When I came to study the phenomenon of spoken testimony, I found many sources of information in the fields of law and religious traditions but a meager minority of philosophical or psychological sources.

The book *"Testimony – A Philosophical Study"* written by C.A.J. Coady (1992) and the book by Felman Shoshana and Laub Dori *"Testimony: The Crisis of Witnessing in Literature, Psychoanalysis, and History"* (1992) stood out for their richness in filling this lacuna and served me as guides through the twists and turns of the epistemology and reliability of spoken testimony.

Why Was Testimony Neglected or – *The Blind Spot in Positive Epistemology*

Testimony and witnessing are (as said, two actions that are one) a daily phenomenon, and very often, everyday phenomena do not challenge academic research. C.A.J. Coady (1992) complains about this tendency and claims that this tradition of neglecting testimony is unjustified and even outrageous, and it may be that testimony has not risen to its proper place due to it being mundane and available to all.[2]

DOI: 10.4324/9781003403920-5

The reason Coady presents is correct, but there are other reasons as well. In what follows, I list very briefly the main ones:

- **Plato** – In order to get to the roots of the reservation about the importance of testimony as a source of knowledge, one must go as far back as Plato, who did not recognize the value of spoken testimony as a good source of knowledge and saw it as inferior in status to perception and memory.
- **Rene Descartes** – A dominant factor in disregarding the words of others was Rene Descartes (1637, 1641), who sought to base human thinking and knowledge as a whole on what an individual himself can know for sure.[3] Descartes worked during the 17th century, and his influence on others' words continued for hundreds of years. It weakened only towards the end of the 20th century, and its traces are still evident today.
- **The separation between rationalism and science** – In addition to these pillars of knowledge, the tendency in the 18th century to separate epistemically between rationalism and science was established. This tendency, which lasted until the second half of the 20th century and, in some ways, exists to this day, underestimates spoken testimonies, which by their very nature, do not rely on scientific research findings.
- **A tendency towards individualism** – This crystallized at the end of the Renaissance period and argued for the rights of the individual, self-autonomy and encouraging personal ability in problem-solving – permeated the values of freedom and human rights, and entered into concepts of knowledge, truth and proof, placing listening to, and trusting in, the words of others – in the shadow.
- **The historical lateness in investigating the act of speech** – A factor that is not mentioned explicitly. This is the historical lateness in investigating the act of speech in general and interpersonal speech in particular. The phenomenon of speech has been studied as a phenomenon in itself only since the end of the 19th century and as a communicative tool even later. Throughout history, humans, in general, have not perceived themselves as beings who 'talk with', and in the course of history, few philosophers regarded speech as a fundamental moment in the life of an individual.[4]

Mikhail Bakhtin (1960) refers to this:

> it is still typical to underestimate, if not altogether ignore, the communicative function of language. Language is regarded from the speaker's standpoint as if there were only one speaker, who does not have any necessary relation to other participants in speech communication.[5]

Heidegger, for example, saw speech as "idle chatter"[6] or as a space in which "an individual lives"[7] rather than as a communicative act.

So, it can be said that the historically late perception of speech as an act in which one individual faces the other also contributed to the neglect of research on spoken testimony.[8]

The Domain of Testimony

In the domain of testimony, there is a distinction between positive and negative epistemology. Both are dominant elements in the testimony space that also delineate its boundaries. This means that, philosophically, both trust and doubt exist in it.

From a philosophical point of view, testimony has an inherent problem that raises the question of how one can justify trusting oral testimony. In other words, what is the epistemological status of a person who delivers a testimony that viewers, or listeners, cannot feel by way of their own senses?

Robin George Collingwood (1970), who wrote the *Map of Knowledge*, claimed that because the foundation for trusting the words of an-other is based on believing what he says, which is not a firm foundation. It can be called a fragile and vulnerable foundation.[9]

This is an inherent problem of spoken testimony that underlies an ongoing philosophical debate surrounding its epistemological status, which marks two main approaches: the 'reductionist' approach, which argues that in order to justify trusting the correctness of testimony, an additional evidence is needed to support its credibility; and the 'non-reductionist' approach, which is broader and justifies trust in testimony, *per se*, by placing the emphasis on the emotional condition of the witness and his intentions.

Three Stations in Time

The status of spoken testimony has undergone a number of turns over the years, and the fluctuations in the recognition of its importance have always been determined in accordance with the dominant world views at any given time. The working assumption here is that when doubt dominates philosophical thinking, the epistemological status of spoken testimony declines.

First Station – Antiquity and the Medieval Period

In ancient times, long before the Cartesian earthquake that created a sharp dichotomy between object and subject, the pursuit of unity and completeness governed the philosophical world.[10] Subjectivity was not considered a hindrance to the credibility of spoken testimony. Trust in others' testimonies was natural.

Even the historian Herodotus (484–425 BC), who was highly trusted and is now considered 'the father of written history', openly stated that he did not only rely on eyewitnesses' accounts but also on travel stories he had heard, on archeological remains and on oral testimonies.[11]

But, to some degree, even then, the paradox controlled the epistemological status of spoken testimony. On the one hand, as mentioned, the evidence enjoyed the value of truth. But on the other hand, in Plato's attempts to build a 'body of knowledge', he preferred perception and memory as good sources of knowledge. Although elsewhere in his writings ("*Theaetitus*"), Plato doubted the credibility of the senses and spoke of the 'illusions of the senses'.

Aristotle thought otherwise. In his book "*Poetics*" he expressed great appreciation for a story and preferred it to the historian:

> The historian and the poet differ from each other, not in what it tells in considered language . . . but in this they differ, that one tells the cases as they were, and the other as they might have been. And therefore, philosophical is the poet and superior to history, dealing with the general while history is the private matter.[12]

To this, Aristotle added his thoughts about the methodology of accumulating knowledge that clearly illustrate his preferred approach to a story.[13]

> There are six ways of "recognitions": (1) Recognition by signs. (2) Recognition invented by the poet. (3) Recognition dependent on memory. (4) Recognition is the process of reasoning. (5) Recognition composite kind of recognition involving false inference on the part of one of the characters. (6) But, of all recognitions, the best is that which arises from the development of the events themselves.[14]

This paradox between great dependence on other testimonies and the lack of scientific appreciation, or the preferred research approach to perception and memory, also appears in medieval philosophy.

Thomas Aquinas (1250) offers a unique and contradictory argument. In his work, Aquinas attempted to combine faith and the desirable rather than trying to separate them.

According to Aquinas, the epistemic status of testimony is "halfway between belief and will".[15] He specifies that there are things in our lives that are far from the senses and can only be validated by trusting in the words of others: "Giving trust and giving credit to the words of others, are the basis for social justice."[16]

Aquinas's argument shifts the weight of the question of the credibility of the act of spoken testimony from the philosophical plane to a different plane, that of faith.

Second Station – The New Era: The 17th and 18th Centuries

During the modern age, the Western world was dominated by positivism, Cartesian thinking[17] and the spirit of the Enlightenment, all of which espoused individualism and the binarism between object and subject, between mind and emotion and between inner and outer. In such an atmosphere, the status of other testimonies has greatly diminished and has been regularly questioned.

In the introduction to Descartes's *"Discourse de la Method", Meditations on the First Philosophy"* (1641), Eran Dorfman writes:

> In the middle of the 17th century, Rene Descartes (1640), during his famous summary in the phrase "I think therefore I Am", ("*Cogito ergo sum*") established the distinction between the thinking object and the expanding object: if thought alone can be the basis for proof existence, it follows that everything which is not characterized by thought, has a dubious existence, and only relying on the good will of God can save it from the jaws of doubt. According to Descartes, the thinking object is the mind, which has the initial certainty, and the expanding object is the body and all other things in the world are null and void beginning with the words of others.[18] This distinction is translated not only into the differences that are obvious but also between – what is and the apparent – that is, between what exists with certainty according to the stated criteria and what only appears to be such but whose existence lacks proof.

In *"Discourse on Method"* (1637), Rene Descartes writes:

> Having decided not to look for more knowledge than that which I could find within myself . . . I decided one day to learn from myself and muster all my mental strength to figure out the ways I should go.[19]

Rene Descartes's thinking influenced the philosophical tradition for hundreds of years, and traces of his ideas are evident to this very day. Even John Lock (1691), who was Descartes's contemporary and had a considerable influence on both philosophy and social thought during that same period, supported this direction of thinking and, in a somewhat absurd way, argued that the views of others contributed nothing, even if it turned out afterwards to be right.[20] About a century later, David Hume (1762) conducted the first serious philosophical discussion on the issue of spoken testimony. Hume was an empiricist in his approach and reluctant to *a priori* trust in other testimonies. Nevertheless, he recognized our daily need for them, and in his book *"A Treatise of Human Nature"* (1748), he emphasized that "There is no species of reasoning more common, more useful, and even more necessary to human life, than that which is derived from the testimonies of men, and the reports of eye-witnesses and spectators."[21]

According to Hume, even though he believed that there is no more efficient source for acquiring information in human life than from the testimonies of others, he claimed that the information given to us from others should be believed only if it is backed by personal experience. In so doing, Hume is considered to be the godfather of the 'reductionist approach', its older form, but also a defender of the personal experience of the other as a good source of knowledge.[22]

In his "*Treatise on Human Nature*" (1739–1740), David Hume offers his appreciation, as well as his reservation, on the subject of testimony.

> To give an instance of this, we may choose any point of history, and consider for what reason we either believe or reject it. Thus, we believe that Caesar was killed in the senate-house on the Ides of March; and that because this fact is established on the unanimous testimony of historians, who agree to assign this precise time and place to that event. Here are certain characters and letters present either to our memory or senses; For even supposing these impressions should be entirely effaced from the memory, the conviction they produced may still remain.[23]

Hume's debate with George Campbell (1762) surrounding the concept of spoken testimony was, in fact, related to a religious discussion about the belief in testimonies of miracles. According to Campbell, testimony precedes experience and has an impact on the person. The initial belief in others' testimonies plays a crucial role in learning and acquiring knowledge. Thomas Reid (1762), who was one of the only important philosophers in European culture, who unreservedly recognized our dependence on other testimonies, supported Campbell and argued that signs (either from perception or from speaking) are previous to experience and they are what cause the listener to trust:

> In the testimony of nature given by the senses, as well as in human testimony, given by language, things are signified to us by signs: and in one, as well as the other, the mind, either by original principles, or by custom, passes from the sign to the conception and belief of the thing signified.
>
> We have distinguished our perceptions into original and acquired, and language, into natural and artificial. Between acquired perception and artificial language, there is a great analogy; but still a greater between original perception and natural language. The signs in original perception are sensations, of which nature hath given us a great variety, suited to the variety of the things signified by them. Nature hath established a real connection between these signs and the things signified, and nature hath also taught us the interpretation of the signs; so that, previous to experience, the sign suggests the thing signified, and creates the belief of it. The signs in natural language are features of the face, gestures of the body, and modulations of the voice.[24]

As evidence of his argument, Reid refers to the developmental stage of children, where trust in testimony has a clear survival dimension. Initial innocence and belief play a crucial role here in a child's normal development and in the acquisition of his knowledge of the world.

In the course of the debate between Hume and Campbell, their positions got closer, and an agreed formula was reached, according to which one can derive knowledge from spoken testimony, unless there is a good reason not to do so.[25]

This agreement is relevant to us because it teaches that Hume was prepared to accept personal testimonies as reliable when they included personal experience, which was a condition that he regarded as important,[26] and testimonies given in psychoanalytical therapy stem from self-experience.

Third Station – 20th and 21st Centuries

The philosophical debate continues.

Yet, this is not the same controversy; things have changed.

Worldviews and moods have changed. After two world wars, the Western world is disappointed with empiricism and has adopted the postmodern ideological position, which has discarded what once were regarded as sacrosanct conventions. At the same time, there was a significant awakening and strengthening of the feminist movement, which by its nature opposes dichotomies and advocates dialogues and reciprocity.

John Austin (1961), for example, wrote that it seems, rather, that believing in other persons in authority and testimony is an essential part of the act of communicating, an act which we all constantly perform. It is as much an irreducible part of our experience as, say, giving promises, or playing competitive games or even sensing colored patches. (*Philosophical Papers*, Chapter 4: "Other Minds" 1979).

In addition, a phenomenon has emerged of a kind of 'longing' for the time when "philosophy was a way of life and not an academic discipline" and a desire to return to ancient thought patterns (Orange 2010), especially in terms of the wish for unification and the willingness for the whole.

This tendency is reflected in the repeated call by philosophical scholars and psychoanalysts to encourage situations of dialogue and elements of reciprocity and to emerge from ideological polarity, as between subject and object, between body and mind, between inside and outside and between control and controlled, dichotomous in which the philosophical and psychological worlds were and are abound.

All of these changed the attitude towards others' testimonies, and the trust in the words of others was strengthened.

Trusting Spoken Testimony

"Believing means liberating the indestructible element in oneself . . .
or, more accurately, being indestructible,
or, more accurately, being"

"Octavo Notebooks", **Kafka, Franz** (1917–1919)[27]

According to Coady (1992), the current controversy does not present a philosophical dichotomy at all. The negative epistemology, he argues, is related to the personal disposition and to the difficulties that have been 'forced' on the philosophical discussion due to the hold of skepticism. "Positive epistemology recognizes skepticism", Coady argues, "but overcomes it and puts doubt to one side."

It can therefore be said that the tendency to believe, or the tendency to doubt, is, more than anything else, indicative of a person's personal disposition.[28] And the ability to believe does not stem from purely external considerations but is, for the most part, a basic and internal element of an individual's personality.

In light of the above and previous deliberations, it seems that the discussion about trusting spoken testimony will not receive an appropriate response if left only to the scientific or rational level but will move between two levels of discussion: between the philosophical plane, to the plane of existential being, and the personal nature of man.

Landmarks in the Current Debate

Landmarks in the ongoing philosophical debate regarding the credibility of spoken testimony are the "affective trust theory", written by Paul Faulkner (2007), and the development of this theory by Tess Dewhurst (2009).

These two researchers attempted to bridge the gap between the 'reductionist' and the 'non-reductionist' approaches by shifting the focus on the issue of trust in testimony from the text to the context, meaning from examining the certainty of statements to the emotional condition of the witness and his intentions.

Paul Faulkner

Faulkner, in his article: "Telling and Trusting" (2007), authored the "Trust theory in testimony". His main argument is that a serious discussion of trust should be on an affective level rather than on an empirical or rational level. According to Faulkner, the ongoing philosophical debate misses the principle that underpins the trust of the recipient, which in his view, lies in the **affective** context. Faulkner attaches crucial importance to the emotional involvement, to the interdependence of and the nature of the relationships that are created between the addresser and the recipient in the communicative process. Thereby giving a prominent place to the subjects themselves.[29]

The question arises – what makes emotional trust logical?

Faulkner explains that the idea that we have a universal epistemic presumption to trust gets the psychology and epistemology of trust wrong. We are not disposed to trust everyone, we only trust certain persons, and cognitively, the relationships are what create the justification for trust.

In his words:

Indeed, there is a tension between acting on trust and acting on evidence that is illustrated in the idea that one does not actually trust someone to do something if one only believes they will do it when one has evidence that they will. However, if trust-based-reasons need not be reasons of evidence, then the existing debate ignores an important possibility. That is, through ignoring the nature of the relationship that audiences can have with speakers, what is missed is the possibility that an audience trusting a speaker can make it reasonable for the audience to accept the trusted speaker's testimony.[30]

Faulkner emphasizes that premature assumptions of skepticism will psychologically and epistemically affect a recipient's trust response. Thus, affective trust has epistemological value, and its justification does not remain on the emotional level alone.[31]

Tess Dewhurst

Dewhurst's theory is based on the 'theory of trust in testimony' of Paul Faukner, but also criticizes it. According to him, the affective variable is not always sufficient.

In his article "The Epistemology of Testimony: Fulfilling the Sincerity Condition" (2009),[32] he points to the act of **intentionality**[33] of the addresser as the decisive variable in giving credence to the testimony as epistemic sincerity'. According to Dewhurst, personal honesty is a necessary condition for the intention to create communication. Dewhurst opposes the idea that the credibility of the witness stems from the relationship formed in the stand of testimony, as Faulkner argued, but the intention of the addresser.

In his words:

The trust theorist is wrong to claim that affective trust is necessary to give a speaker reason to be sincere. However, I believe that the trust view of testimony is right to claim that intentionality plays an important role in our coming to accept testimony as sincere. I will argue that a speaker's reason to be sincere is entailed in having a reason to assert anything at all. If we recognize that a speaker's intention is to communicate, rather than to produce, or bring about, a certain belief in the hearer (as the trust theorist would have it), then there is no longer a need for affective trust to play a role. Sincerity is entailed in having a reason to communicate or share a belief, and thus a hearer is entitled to presume that a speaker is being sincere[34] . . .

Communication is the means by which we share our beliefs. Communication is not simply about causing another person to believe something, but about transmitting information, passing on information that the speaker believes to be true.[35]

This argument raises the following question: does intention have the power to influence the content of the testimony?

Sokolowski responds simply: "Speech will not be credible if we do not mean to be credible."[36]

John Searle

An even more satisfactory explanation is found in Searl's linguistic theory (1983).

Intention, according to Searl, is the key to understanding speech actions.[37] Unlike Brentano and Husserl,[38] Searl argued that the act of intentionality is not entirely consciousness.

Dorit Lemberger (2012) refers to the exploration of Searle's intentionality:

> Searle's important innovation is his pragmatic discussion of the act of intention, which precedes and is expressed in the act of speech . . . The intention dictates the power and the content of the actions of speech . . . thus it is possible to indicate a causal connection between the intention and the action of speech.[39]

If so, the claim of the connection between the intention that precedes the testimony and the speech itself is a legitimate claim, also epistemologically. It establishes trust in others' testimonies when the addresser's intention is to create communication and share his testimony.

List of References and Notes

1 Lackey, Jennifer. (2009): *Learning from Words: Testimony as a Source of Knowledge*. Oxford University Press, Oxford.

2 Coady, Cecil Anthony John (1992): *Testimony: A Philosophical Study*. Clarendon Press, Oxford, England, p. 8.

3 In his essay "Optics" (1637) Rene Descartes reduced man's connection with the world to a concept called "Cartesian", in line with Descartes's Latin name. Descartes formulated a clearer formulation of his ideas in his book *"Meditations on First Philosophy"* (1641) in which he questions everything beyond the realm of rational examination by man.

4 Sagi, Avi (2012): *Facing Others and Otherness: The Ethics of Inner Retreat*. Bar Ilan University Press, Ramat Gan, Israel, pp. 91–96 (Hebrew).

5 Bakhtin, Mikhail Mikhailovich Bakhtin (1986): *Speech Genres and Other Late Essays*. University of Texas Press, Austin, TX. Slavic Series no. 8, p. 10.

6 Heidegger, Martin (1962): *Being and Time*. Harper & Row, New York, p. 197.

7 Heidegger, Martin (1982): *Basic Problems of Phenomenology*. Indiana University Press, Bloomington, IN, p. 120.

8 In this context, Avi Sagi (2012) cites Karl Jaspers and Charles Taylor as exceptions who drew attention to communicative speech and its implications; Jaspers in his book *"Philosophy"*, in the chapter "Communication" and Taylor in his book: *"Philosophy and the Humanities"*.

9 Collingwood, Robin George (1970): *Speculum Mentis or The Map of Knowledge*. Oxford University Press, Oxford.

10 The desire for unity in ancient times is also found in the myths created at that time, such as in the story of the creation of the biblical (first) world: *"Male and female he created them"* (Genesis 1:27) or: *"And he clung to his wife and they became one flesh"*, (Genesis 2:24). And even more in the legend of the "Eros and the Three Sexes in Plato's Symposium 'Third Sex'" (Plato, 385 B.C.) In ancient times, humans were divided into

three species . . . The third sex was a fusion of the male and the female. "They angered the gods and Zeus cut them in half, "and since then each of us is always looking for the other part of himself." Although on closer inspection there is a significant difference here when "the biblical model of existence is aimed at 'being with the other'" while "the human model of existence is of a single person who achieves the perfection of his being as a single person" (Sagi 2009, p. 25), but the desire for unification is evident in both.

11 Herodotus (1920): *Histories* (424–430 BC), trans. A. D. Godley. Harvard University Press, Cambridge, MA (1998).

12 Aristotle's thoughts are relevant to us because spoken testimony is a certain kind of story.

13 Aristotle (c 335 B.C.) (1997): *Poetics*. Dover Publications Inc, New York, p. 16.

14 Ibid., p. 82.

15 Thomas Aquinas (end of 1250's) "*Commentary on Boetinus's De Trinitate*", in C.A.Z. Coady (1992), p. 16.

16 Ibid., p. 17.

17 In his essay "*Optics*" (1637) Descartes reduced man's connection with the world to a concept called "Cartesian", taken from Descartes's Latin name, a clearer formulation of his conception by Descartes in his book "*Meditations on First Philosophy*" (1641) in which he questions everything beyond the realm of rational examination of man.

18 Dorfman, Eran (2008): *What Path in Life Shall I Follow? Introduction to the Hebrew Translation of Descartes, R. Discourse on Method*. Carmel, Jerusalem, p. 9 (Hebrew).

19 Descartes, Rene (1637): *Discourse on Method*, Published By Rene Descartes. Discourse de la méthode, French.
    Herodotus. *Histories* (424–430 BC), 1998.

20 Lock, John (1689): *An Essay Concerning Human Understanding*, ed. John W. Yolton. T. Tegg and Son publishing, Original from: Oxford University, London (1961), p. 58.

21 Hume, David (1739–40): *A Treatise of Human Nature* (1748), ed. David Fate Norton Mary J. Norton, Volume 1: Texts Clarendon Press. Published in the United States by Oxford University Press Inc., New York (2007), pp. 80–84.

22 Hume, David (1748). *An Enquiry Concerning Human Understanding*, ed. T. L. Beauchamp. Oxford University Press, Oxford (2000).

23 Hume, David (1739–40), pp. 80–84.

24 Thomas, Reid (2017): *Essays on the Intellectual Powers of Man: An Inquiry into the Human Mind on the Principles of Common Sense; and an Essay on Quantity*. First published 2000; substantive revision, 2014 (Locations 12609 to 12620). Harvard Press, Cambridge, MA.

25 Hume (1748), in: Livingston (1984), p. 232.

26 Ibid.

27 Kafka, Franz (1917–1919): *The Blue Octavo Notebooks*. Max Brod. Exact Change Publishing, Cambridge, MA, 1991 (ISBN 1-878972-04-9) (1953), p. 27.

28 Coady, Cecil Anthony John (1992), p. 8.

29 Faulkner, Paul (2007): "On Telling and Trusting". *Mind*, 116 (464), pp. 875–905.

30 Ibid., p. 876.

31 Ibid.

32 Dewhurst, Tess (2009): "The Epistemology of Testimony: Fulfilling the Sincerity Condition". *South African Journal of Philosophy*, Rhodes University, Grahamstown, 6139, South Africa, 28 (2), pp. 93–101.

33 It should be noted that the meaning of the concept of intentionality, which Tess Dewhurst refers to, is an intention to act in a certain way, that it is an act that belongs to a person's field of activity as opposed to 'phenomenological intentionality'. Some argue that these concepts should be termed differently and called 'phenomenological intentionality' or aboutness.

34 Ibid., p. 94.

35 Ibid., p. 98.
36 Sokolowski, R. (1974): *"Phenomenology Is about Truth and Reason": The Formation of Husserl's Concept of Constitution.* Northwestern University Press, Evanston (1974), p. 3.
37 Searle, John (1983): *Intentionality.* Cambridge University Press, Cambridge, pp. 160–166.
38 Searle's concept is different from the concept of phenomenological intentionality, which is a mental structure, it is a mental act that belongs, according to Brentano and Husserl (1952, pp. 138–152), to the field of consciousness, a mental ability directed to speech. Mental states, such as thoughts, beliefs, hopes or intentions and basically any longing or hope, are always directed to a particular object, including these, and also the intention to say something or act in a certain way.
39 Lemberger, Dorit (2012): *Twenty-Four Readings in Aharon Appelfeld's Literary Work.* Bar Ilan University, Ramat Gan; Shalom Hartman Institute, Jerusalem (2011), pp. 86–87.

Chapter 5

Types of Spoken Testimony

Zipi Rosenberg Schipper

Introduction

Spoken testimony is given in three forms:

Formal testimony – which is legal testimony or historical testimony.
Natural testimony – which is testimony given daily from person to person or through the media.
Personal testimony – which is a person's testimony about himself.

The concept of spoken testimony is inherently a diffuse concept, but the legal world is confronted with it by laws and rules that shape it more tightly than other contexts, and therefore it is good to start with it.

Legal Testimony

Of all the issues related to the testimony given in court, I chose to dwell on the historical evolution of the laws of witnessing and giving testimony, dealing between a person and the other and between a person and himself, beginning with the biblical laws, through the Halakhic laws, to the Hebrew law and the law of the state of Israel.

The Sources of Legal Testimony

All the laws of witnesses and legal testimony originate in the Scriptures.

What follow are the main verses in the Bible (Tanakh)[1] that are the sources of the laws of testimony between people, and between man and himself, according to their subjects:

An honest witness – "*A true witness delivereth souls*" (Proverbs 14:25).
A faithful witness – "*will not lie; but a false witness breatheth forth lies*" (Proverbs 14:5).
A false witness – "*You shall not bear false witness against your neighbor*" (Exodus 20:12).

DOI: 10.4324/9781003403920-6

A malicious witness – "*put not thy hand with the wicked to be an unrighteous witness*" (Exodus 23:1). "*Be not a witness against thy neighbor without cause; and deceive not with thy lips*" (Proverbs 24:28).

All of these are epithets for a witness who comes to testify wrongfully and misleadingly.

The Duty to Testify – "*And if any one sin, in that he heareth the voice of adjuration, he being a witness, whether he hath seen or known, if he do not utter it, then he shall bear his iniquity*" (Leviticus 5:1).

The Duty to Tell the Truth – "*Be not a witness against thy neighbor without cause; and deceive not with thy lips*" (Proverbs 24:28). "*Let them bring their witnesses, that they may be justified*" (Isaiah 43:9).

Eye Witnessing – the preferable testimony is eye-witnessing. After it, the preference is testimony heard firsthand. Whoever did not see the act but heard the testimony from others is a "*witness of a witness*" (Sanhedrin 4:5).

"A witness cannot be a judge" (Rosh Hashanah, 20); whoever comes to testify in a certain trial cannot be the judge and prosecute the accused.

Sages of blessed memory have pondered over these Biblical verses from numerous angles and created a multiplicity of laws that are concentrated in various files. The "Tractate of Testimony" is one of the important files, listing eight topics that will be detailed below, followed by the commandments of testimony relating to the 'does and don'ts' of certain actions.

What follows is an expansion of the main categories of witnessing and giving testimony and their development from the days of the Mishnah and the Talmud through Jewish law to the contemporary Israeli law.

Laws and 'Halakhot' Relating to a Witness and a Testimony

In the words of the sages of blessed memory, testimony reflects everything said by the witness.

Tractate of Testimonies

This tractate is part of "Sefer Nezikin" (Damages), to be found in the fourth of the six books of the Mishna. It includes matters that were testified in front of the judges.[2] And its halakhot are assembled from the entire Mishna.

It Consists of Eight Chapters

(1) The duty to testify – The meaning of refraining from giving testimony and enforcing it.

(2) <u>Denied testimony</u> – Testimony against which there is evidence that denies Babylonian Talmud (Baba Batra 31:1).

(3) <u>Intentional testimony</u> – A testimony without defect – Babylonian Talmud (Baba Batra 168:2).

(4) <u>Evidence that there is no possibility</u> that other witnesses will come and initiate it; invalid (Sanhedrin 41:1).

(5) <u>Testimony that has been partially nullified</u> or completely nullified (Baba Kamma 73:1).

(6) <u>Conspiring witnesses</u> – Witnesses found guilty of plotting and then found guilty of lying. Rabbi Yoḥanan said, "*falsehood, falsehood*" (Jerusalem Talmud Makkot 1 1:6).

(7) <u>Palginan Dibora</u> – A situation in which the court chooses from testimony part of what has been said.

(8) <u>Commandments (mitzvot) of Do or Don't Do</u>

The Halakhot of testimony, in general, talks of eight testimonial commandments, three commandments "to do" and five commandments "not to do".[3]

Three Testimonial Commandments to Do

(1) The commandment that whoever has evidence must testify in Court.[4]
(2) The commandment to ask and investigate the witnesses.[5]
(3) The commandment to do to the conspiratorial witness as he did.[6]

Five Commandments Not to Do

(4) That the witness is not allowed to testify in a trial of one who testified against him in the 'law of souls'.
(5) That nothing be done on the basis of one witness.
(6) That an offender is not allowed to testify.
(7) That a relative is not allowed to testify.
(8) Not to testify falsely.

Five main categories emerge from these categories (mitzvot), which are relevant to the image of the concept of spoken testimony in the legal domain, as well as in the social and personal realms.

The categories are the duty to testify, a warning against false testimony, no person can consider himself evil, between legal testimony and factual testimony and witnesses and judges.

The Categories in Detail

The Duty to Testify[7]

> "*And if any one sin, in that he heareth the voice of adjuration, he being a witness, whether he hath seen or known, if he does not utter it, then he shall bear his iniquity;*"
>
> Leviticus 5:1

This is the verse from which the sages learned about the duty of testifying. The conceptual basis underlying this duty, according to Maimonides – to be found in the Book of "Mitzvot" – is part of the overriding principle of brotherhood and mutual help between human beings.[8]

The question that arises is: "What happens to those who refrain from testifying; does this have judicial consequences?"

There is a controversy surrounding this question: Rabbi Yehoshua (The Babylonian Talmud) explains that:

> He who knows testimony that another has a use for, is obligated to testify. If he withholds his testimony, he is exempt from judgement by man but is liable by the laws of the heavens[9]

On the other hand, in the 13th century in Spain, Maimonides argued that he who refrains from testifying is free to do so, that he had no financial obligation other than that, and if he does not want to bother himself and testify, he is under no obligation.

Although God is always outside any equation of law or judgment, the ruling that "The man is exempt from judgement by man, but is liable by the laws of the heavens"[10] is completely unique and does not exist in any legal system,

A Warning Against False Testimony[11]

The commandment forbidding false testimony is stated twice in the Bible using differing linguistic terms. The first is in the "Ten Commandments"[12] in the Book of Exodus: "*You shall not bear false witness against your neighbor*" (Exodus 20:13), and the second is in Deuteronomy: "*You shall not bear false witness against your neighbor*" (Deuteronomy 5:17).

Despite these expressly worded commandments, false testimony has never been eradicated.

In the Hebrew law, someone who testifies falsely about his friend can be found to have caused not only indirect but direct damage because his testimony is responsible for directly harming the victim. If the damage is indeed caused both indirectly or directly, the witness who lied may have to compensate the victim financially.

In the Israeli law, opinions are divided, mainly due to the diminishing power of testimonies.

Conspiring Witnesses

Conspiring witnesses are witnesses whose testimony has been negated (Makkot 2:2). This is to say that after these witnesses had testified, two other witnesses testified that at the time of the incident on which the testimony was based, they were the first people to arrive at the location and were unable to see any such incident.

The outcome of the deed is prescribed in Deuteronomy: "*You shall do to the one as the one schemed to do to the other*" (Deuteronomy 19:19)

The Hebrew law emphasizes that in cases of conspiring witnesses, he who owes a sum of money is obligated to pay the victim and not to the public coffers.

In Israeli law, false testimony and conspiring witnesses are within the bounds of committing a criminal offense.

Between Man and Himself

"No man calls himself evil"

(Talmudic Encyclopedia Volume 1, p. 189)

The Gemara explains: Rava says, "A person is his own relative and so a person cannot make himself wicked. Consequently, the part of the testimony that relates to the witness's own status is not accepted" (Sanhedrin 25a). This means that no individual can testify against himself, be that for his own benefit or to his detriment. Because for a relative to testify, for or against himself, is invalid.

But if a person has acquired the reputation of an evil person, for example: if a person testifies that he has lent with interest and another person testifies that that was indeed the case, the second witness's testimony would be accepted as a basis for conviction.

There are those who object and say that the rule that no person considers himself evil applies to the matter of testimony only.

Between Factual Truth and Legal Truth[13]

The wisest of linguists, including the sages of Hebrew law, thought on the connection – in Hebrew – between the word 'testimony' (edut) and the word 'more' (od) and interpreted that there is in the testimony a revival of the event, on which the testimony is given as if it were recurring.

The Hebrew law bestowed great power to witnesses and their testimony. As a result, in cases of evidence that supported the defendant's acquittal, even if the judge were to believe that the factual findings raised a reasonable concern about the crime having been committed, he had to acquit the defendant. Mainly, for this reason, there were strict provisions regarding the eligibility of witnesses and the procedures required for the collection of their testimony.

In general, spoken testimony serves as strong proof of legal validity but not necessarily proof of factual truth. In this context, the question of the difference between legal and factual testimony arises.

The gap between factual truth and halakhic or legal truth – as expressed by the judges' conclusions – that is accepted within the limitations of the law of evidence is a question that runs like a common thread in all legal history and is resolved in line with the mood of the times. In the Hebrew law, it was resolved by giving priority to the testimonies of witnesses; not so in the Israeli law.

For example: Judge Elon addressed (1982) the issue of factual truth versus legal truth when the question arose as to whether there was any point in setting up a commission of inquiry into the assassination of Haim Arlosorov decades after his murder.

The court, which relied extensively on the sources of the Hebrew law on this issue, rejected the petitioner's argument and ruled that there was no justification for establishing the committee.

In Judge Elon's words:

> Any conclusion reached by the Commission of Enquiry does not, and cannot, presume to change from the legal truth set forth in the Court's ruling. But the commission of inquiry may come and presume to attempt to arrive at the means of inquiry and evidence that is presented to it, investigate the factual truth, which is not necessarily consistent with the legal truth.[14]

The Question of Truth and the Protection of Human Rights

On the issue of the protection of human rights, the difference in the law of testimony between Jewish law and the Israeli legal system is clear.

In Israeli law, as in other Western, modern legal systems, quite a few basic laws have been enacted concerning the values of human dignity and liberty, which have the potential to make it difficult to arrive at the study of factual truth and to impair it. For example, the rule prohibiting the receipt of evidence obtained in an illegal manner does not exist in the Halakhic laws of testimony. There is also an avoidance of information for the purpose of protecting social values[15] or security issues.

In addition, in the Israeli law, which does not give such power to testimonies, restrictions on the invalidity of testimony, such as individual testimony, female testimony, testimony of relatives and evidence related to belongings, which existed in the Jewish legal system and sometimes made it difficult to discover the factual truth, were removed. As a result, the status of legal truth rose.

Witnesses and Judges[16]

There was, and still is, a clear distinction between witnesses and judges: "No witness becomes a judge".[17] The role of the witnesses is to testify about what happened, and the role of the judges is to rule on the case. A Witness Acting as Judge (Negative Commandment, 291): "*But one witness shall not testify against a person causing him to die*" (Numbers 35:30).

> In a capital case, a witness may not offer any opinion regarding the defendant's guilt or innocence. Rather, he must state the facts as he saw them and then remain silent, and allow the judges to reach their decision.[18]

But a careful study of the Hebrew law reveals that the separation between witnesses and judges in Hebrew law was mainly on the personal level and less on the substantive level.

In the Hebrew law, the purpose of the witness was not only to convince the judges of the truth of the testimony, but more than that: when the judges hear the testimony, they must rule according to it.

In Maimonides's view:

> There is no sentencing tribunal except by witnesses with clear evidence . . . Who were ordered to settle the matter according to two witnesses, even though we do not know whether they testified truthfully or falsely.[19]

The culmination of this method was expressed in an extreme way when in addition to their 'classical' role, witnesses were given the task of carrying out the sentence imposed, as was written "*Let the hands of the witnesses be the first to put [the condemned] to death*" (Deuteronomy 17:7).

The halakha that it was up to witnesses to carry out the sentencing was learned from this verse. Maimonides wrote the reason for this:

> And you already knew that the witnesses are the ones who testify what kind of death it will be, since the same thing is true with them, which they obtained with their senses, and it is with us a story of things, which we do not know except what we heard from them (from the witnesses). And therefore, God, blessed be He, commanded that the witnesses should be in charge of the matter.[20]

The reason for this lies in the great significance that the Sages attributed to witnesses experiencing directly, with their own senses, what they are testifying to.[21]

These things have changed.

The central status of witnesses and their testimony has diminished in modern legal systems. In Hebrew law, a "formal assessment method" was accepted, and in the modern system, a "free assessment method" is practiced.

In Israeli law, the separation between witnesses and judges is carefully maintained, and no witness ever becomes a judge.

It should be noted that all the developments of the legal aspects of spoken testimony presented here indicate, more than anything, the changing values of society over time. Also, it is emphasized that all five of the categories discussed, which actually encompass most of the aspects of legal testimony, are not limited to legal aspects but constitute connotations that exist in any type of spoken testimony. For example, legal testimony – measured by its power to reach a judgment but is not necessarily a factual truth, nor is the question of whether the testimony corresponds to reality or is essentially false – exists in all types of testimony. Also, the principle of the obligation to testify, that the idea behind it is for the mutual help and good of society, is a recurring idea in any type of testimony, and this is especially evident in the testimonies that are given in the study of the Holocaust.

Natural Testimony

"There are things in our lives that are far from the senses, and can only be validated from trusting in the words of others, 'giving trust and giving credit to the words of others are the basis for social justice.'"[22]

Thomas Aquinas (1250)

A person encounters 'natural' testimony on a daily basis. Natural evidence provides information through human-to-human communication. C.A.J. Coady (1992) called it "The social operations of mind."[23] The moniker "natural" was given to this type of testimony by Thomas Reid (1674). Natural testimony has no special rules or morals. We rely on natural testimony all the time, even if it is clear to us that, in most cases, there is no first-hand testimony. On the contrary, all the information we tend to get, such as recommendations about things we consume in different areas of life, or even guidance in unknown ways, or in media broadcasts on various topics, for the most part, are not first-hand.

In many cases, these are events from distant places; all the information about them is related to a chain of testimonies.

Recently (1968), it was even decided in the English law to accept hear-say testimony as admissible in court under certain conditions.[24]

Natural, everyday testimonies are mostly statements that provide general information, although natural testimonies given personally are sometimes of a personal nature. In this, they are similar to personal testimonies concerning the subject himself, and like them, they have a high emotional involvement.

Yet, natural testimony is by its nature monologic and by that, it is more similar to legal testimony.

Personal Testimony

"I still believe that every real spiritual matter should be viewed through a personal prism."

"Essays in the First Person", **Appelfeld, Aharon** (1978)

Introduction: In describing personal testimony, this book moves from formal definitions to observing the essence of the phenomenon.

Spoken personal testimony is always of a person, about himself.

From a historical point of view, personal testimony is, as said, fundamentally the phenomenon of the martyr, the witness of faith, who embodies his testimony in his body.

A close look at the image of personal testimony reveals that the connotations which characterized the martyr phenomenon, such as suffering, self-risk, personal sacrifice, high emotional involvement and even the embodiment of testimony in the body, are inserted in the concept of personal testimony and characterize it, to this day.

Personal testimony is sometimes accompanied by a certain behavior that indicates the feelings of the testifier. Also, there are testimonies that the very act of listening is not always easy and sometimes involves suffering (Felman and Laub (1992), Orange (1995) and Aron (2011)).

However, unlike the martyr, whose testimony is always given through deeds, spoken personal testimony is essentially a practice of words.

Etymological support for this claim is also obtained from the English language, in which the idea of suffering is an immanent part of the literal term itself – "bearing witness". This brings us to the two stages of testimony.

Personal testimony, like all testimonies, has a double meaning (testimony and witnessing), which are basically two stages. It starts with a real occurrence, which the addresser witnessed, and afterwards becomes an inner experience, which by its very nature, is beyond time and place. The second stage is speaking the experience.

Unlike other testimonies, personal testimony does not end with the story of the occurrence and, in fact, is dependent on the presence of an-other who is attentive and responsive. This gives the testimony a dialogical structure. The recipient's attention is a unique form of attention, which is characterized by a presence that does not aspire to sovereignty.

In giving personal testimony, the recipient becomes a witness of a witness. It can be described as an action in which one person observes another one speaking about an event, of which he was not a part, and becomes cognitively and emotionally involved in it.

The second stage is a phase of healing. It gives existence to an internal experience and thus validates it. This way, the testimony is given a different status for the testifier, which is usually easier to bear.

At this point, the role of the recipient is emphasized, which is, in fact, the factor that distinguishes the action of personal testimony from other testimonies. In legal testimony, the recipient's sovereignty does not change, and in natural testimony, which is informative by its nature, the recipient's sovereignty does not play a role.

The task of the recipient in personal testimony is to be an attentive and believing, what let the testimony come into being.

The sociologist Irving Goffman (1997) attached great importance to the role of the recipient witness in the self-establishment of an individual. In the postmodern conception that he expresses, the 'self' is its various manifestations, and the manifestation in the presence of a witness is an act of self-establishment.

The recipient, as a witness to the testimony, also changes and undergoes a process, which is the nature of a dialogue, since not only the speaking self comes to consciousness, but the recipient also comes to consciousness, and by being there, he is a partner in the becoming and shaping of the testimony.

On the Transition Between the Two Stages of Testimony and the Inner Witness

The transition from the first to the second stage in personal testimony is natural and desirable, but this is not always the case. Sometimes there are impasses that do not allow any transition

Felman and Laub (1992) write, "To bring one to the other side of language, one must first come out on the other side of death: one must survive, in order to bear witness."[25]

Paul Celan (1994) addressed this point in his own unique poetic way:

He who goes with his very being into language, reality-wounded and reality-seeking[26]

Special reference to the difficulty of moving to the second stage is provided by Dana Amir (2013). According to her, a person's inability to testify is related to an inner injury in what Amir calls the "testimonial function in the psyche."[27] This function creates a kind of reactive blockage to ongoing difficult events and paralyzes the subject's ability to tell a story that will, in effect, catch up with his own history.

The 'witnessing function in the psyche', according to Amir, is the function of giving validity to the experience of the self. This function is not only related to the individual's ability to observe himself but also to his ability to testify to it.

We are talking about a function that develops "in response to a tolerable level of the baby being 'helpless', and in the face of a satisfying experience of the baby being observed by a third presence – that of the father, or another third".[28]

In a similar way, Amir argues that the function of the internal witness can be developed in an adult by an external witness, such as a caregiver or therapist who serves as an external observer, present when the testimony is given.

Moore (1999) also addressed this issue and argued that we know that an event occurred to us only when the other provides a narrative for it because only the other, the external witness, is the one who gives a person first-hand knowledge.[29]

When Does Testimony Becomes a Psychic Moment?

Agamben (1998), who saw testimony as being in the space between – someone who has a voice but has nothing to say and someone who has a lot to say but has no voice – teaches us when spoken testimony becomes a mental psychic moment.

A 'psychic moment' is formed when a person does not own a significant experience that he went through, and a state of a lack of validity of the same experience is created.

The lack of internal or external approval for significant or prolonged experiences a person endures is sometimes experienced as a developmental lag. Sándor Ferenczi compared this lack to 'fragmentation'.[30] Michael Balint (1968) described it as a "psychic break"[31] in the continuous development of life, which may lead to impairment and decline in daily function. Dealing with such situations is sometimes done through a waiver of inner uniformity, as termed by Ferenczi: "The easy thing to do is to destroy to us the rule that unites the mental images into one unity".[32]

In Agamben's opinion, this 'lacuna' usually causes daily functioning that has the characteristics of a split. A split that will only be bridged by acquiring the missing story.

Spoken testimony enables this acquisition to take place and thereby builds a bridge over the gap created between contemporary life and what was. This is very evident in the experience of an immigrant or in the experience of the returning prisoner and also in a person after a long physical or psychiatric hospitalization who needs a witness to the story of his life 'there' and the story of his life 'here'.

The Element of Construction in Spoken Testimony and the Questions It Arouses

Every spoken testimony goes through construction. Every testimony tells its story from the end to the beginning, which means that the construction is an inherent element in spoken testimony.

Felman and Laub (1992) refer to this:

Verbal acts consist of *someone telling someone else that something happened.* That "something happened". Someone is telling – is a story, someone is telling someone else that something happened – is history, and both become united in the discourse of testimony, which mediates between narrative and history.[33]

(Italics in the original.)

Within the statement that spoken testimony connects history and narration, there is already the assumption that every testimony undergoes construction.[34]

This assumption raises questions about the bearing of the witness's responsibility for what he saw or experienced, which becomes a moral question in the person-to-person relationship.

This question also carries a moral political charge towards the close or far society, whether a person sees himself as belonging to it or whether he sees society surrounding him as alien to him.

Additional questions also arise in this context: "Is it at all possible to treat the testimony of the witness as 'authentic' testimony?"; "Does the fact that he was present at the event really bring him closer to 'truth'?"; or, as has often been claimed, "Does being at the scene, close to what is happening, hide the 'big picture' from him and limit his understanding of the event?"; or, on the other hand, "What is the validity of a testimony given after a while; could it obscure and weaken the memory of the witness or vice versa?"; and "What is the judgment of testimony given for the second and third time? Is the repetition of the testimony a guarantee of the preservation of the story, or rather for its change?"

Primo Levi, in his book *"The Drowned and the Saved"* (1986), tries to answer some of these questions:

> Human memory is a wonderful but fallible instrument. This hackneyed truth is known not only to psychologists but also to anyone who has paid attention to his own behaviour or that of the people around him. The memories residing within us are not engraved in stone. Not only do they tend to fade over the years; they often change or even grow to incorporate extraneous features, by adding foreign characters. . . . The limited reliability of our memories will be explained satisfactorily only once we know in what language and in what alphabet they are written, on what material and with what type of pen; this goal is still distant today . . . Frequent recollection definitely keeps a memory fresh and alive . . . But a memory that is recollected too often, and expressed in the form of a story, tends to harden into a stereotype, a tried-and-true formula, crystallized, perfected, adorned, that installs itself in the place of the raw memory and grows at its expense.[35]

"Memory Materials Emerge and Rise from the Body"[36] – The Influence of the Martyr

To reinforce the far-reaching influence of the phenomenon of the martyr on the nature of personal testimony today, I will cite a number of quotations by researchers who have been engaged with this subject.

In the analysis of Camus's book *"The Plague"* (1947), to Felman and Laub (1992), the influence of the martyr phenomenon is clearly visible:

> It is thus that the literary testimony of *"The Plague"* offers its historical eye witnessing in the flesh . . . an experience that requires one to live through one's own death, and paradoxically, bear witness to that living through one's dying. A death experience which can be truly comprehended, witnessed only from inside (from inside the witness' own annihilation), a radical experience to which no outsider can be witness, but to which no witness can be, or remain, outsider.[37]

Referring to another book by Camus, *"The Fall"* (1956), Felman and Laub bring up the image of the martyr as Jesus's allegorical image:

> Since the witness can, by definition, have no ally, Christ in turn is betrayed by his own allies, and his testimony, met by deafness and repressed by silence, is ironically denied by his own apostles.[38]

In the underground magazine "Combat" (1948), Camus himself published an article in this spirit about the role of the artist in historical testimonies:

> The role of the artist is to shatter the false image of history **as an abstraction in being a witness to the body** . . . the artist's destiny is to be witness of the freedom – not of the law, but witness of the flesh.
>
> (Emphasis in original.)

Sagi (2009) also refers to this issue, and its wording appears in the title of the paragraph – "The memory materials emerge and rise from the body itself. The memory itself is expressed in the body and is a kind of photo album of the memory."[39]

Indeed, the ancient religious practices, which remained on the physical plane and on the plane of deeds, are still influential, yet, as said, there is a caveat: the concept of personal testimony chose the path of the words.

The contents of the personal testimony are steeped in high emotional involvement, and its focus is on himself. But the verbal practice of speaking testimony that outlines a dialogical framework of addresser and recipient has moved away from the realization of testimony in deeds and also from the person being alone with his testimony.

Each Poem Is a Testimony

Heidegger's linguistic theory taught us about the power of the word in the presence of the spoken experience. It can be said that testimony is validated not because it is rational or empirically valid but because of the recipient's ability to experience the spoken occurrence and the addresser's ability to re-experience it through the presence that speech establishes.[40]

In this context, Buber writes in the introduction to his book "*The Hidden Light*" (1969):

> The matter of the story is more than just an act of speech, it actually conveys what happened . . . an event that is told about, intensified anew, a force that acted before, fruitful in living speech.[41]

Heidegger's linguistic statement (1978), which marks the moment when speech itself succeeds in presenting the object of speech, was directed primarily at poetic speech.

In his words:

> The moment when language is exposed in its being, is when the verbal language stops and cannot find the appropriate word to describe the experience it seeks to express.[42]

And elsewhere:

> The moment when we have difficulty finding the right word for something that interests us . . . or when we are left without the ability to say what is in our mind

. . . it is a moment when language itself, at a distance and transiently, touches us in its very being.[43]

This poetic utterance is the characteristic of testimony, which has its own rhythm, which very often has to search for an appropriate word, which is sometimes stuttering and sometimes hesitant. It often happens in testimony, as Heidegger puts it, that language speaks through us, and we allow it to say what it tells us.[44]

The somewhat surprising parallel made here, between the characteristics of poetic speech and verbal characteristics of testimony, is not entirely unfounded. Poets such as Paul Celan (1994) reinforce this view, and in his speech on the occasion of receiving the Breman City Prize for Literature (1958), he said that every poem is a testimony.[45]

In his words (translated by poet Rosmarie Waldrop).

A poem is a manifest form of language and thus inherently dialogue. It may be a letter in a bottle sent out to sea with the hope (not always greatly hopeful) that it may somehow, somewhere and sometime, wash up on land, on heartland perhaps;

. . .

Poems in this sense are always under way, they are making toward something. Toward what? Toward something standing open, occupiable, perhaps toward a "thou" that can be addressed, to an addressable reality[46]

For the poem is not timeless, it is immersed in reality and in time. It claimes the infinite but through time, not circumventing time. In poetry the contemporary is engraved, it remembers its dates, it has a present and a presence in it. Such poetry is not monolinguistic, but dialogic, yearning for the other.[47]

This sentence is a beautiful articulation of poetry. But of spoken testimony too. As the poet first meets a poem as a living thing made not of language but of sensations and then dresses them with language, so is a testimony and as the poet releases the poem into the world the poem, seeks a reader, an audience, so is a testimony

It ment a movement, you see, something, being *un route*, an attempt to find a direction.

whenever I ask about the sense of it, I remined myself that this implys as which sense is clockwise. In poetry the contemporary is engraved, it remembers its dates, it has a present and a presence in it. Such poetry is not monolinguistic, but dialogic, yearning for the other.[48]

Paul Celan is not the only one who sees the song as a testimony; Yehuda Amichai, as another example, often talked about a poem, or a song, as a testimony to life. As in his article: "My Judaism":

This is the essence of poetry: personal documentation, a living museum, in which the poet commemorates from his life. In a love song, for example, there are parts of sentences, words, objects, clothes, furniture, hills, etc., which help the poet preserve his life beyond time and place and sustain them beyond their corporality.[49]

And there are many others.

Is Personal Testimony a Dialogue?

Personal testimony differs from other testimonies in that its essence addresses a recipient, knowing that the recipient is present and responding.

Felman and Laub (1992) emphasized that "Testimonies are not monologues; they cannot take place in solitude."[50]

This procedural sequence places it as a dialogical discourse. The dialogical basic pattern of personal testimony is not only a framework of rules, but is a constitutive function in the development of its contributive value.

Examining the characteristics of the dialogue and of the monologue teaches us that spoken personal testimony is indeed, for the most part and in its essence, dialogical speech. It embraces a majority of the characteristics of the dialogue: it begins with an occurrence and continues with a verbal event; it contains changes in the experiences of those who participate in it – the addressor, the addressee and the testimony itself – and there is mutual trust, mutual absorption and mutual respect for those who participate in the discourse.

Yet, a careful analysis of the characteristics of the monologue versus the dialogue shows that spoken personal testimony does not fully meet the criteria of a dialogical discourse and has at least two significant elements that go beyond this discourse and belong to the category of a monologue: one – is the hierarchical relationship between the partners in the situation; and two – is the maintenance of the sovereignty addressee in the discourse.

Theoretically, this particular reservation is justified, yet the practice of personal testimony and the experience in the clinical field show that the position of testimony on the continuum between dialogue and monologue is much closer to the first.

That reinforces what has already been said, that in any attempt to find a theoretical anchor for spoken testimony, it seems that from a philosophical point of view, it is always positioned in intermediate spaces, like a bridge holding two poles,

Trusting Personal Testimony

We know from the previous discussion (see page 40) that dealt with the question of trust in testimony in general, that the tendency to believe, or the tendency to doubt is, more than anything else, indicative of a person's personal disposition. Also similar to what was said in that previous debate, the search for a justification of trust in testimony will not receive a satisfactory answer only on the epistemological level but will move between the philosophical plane and the plane of a human being. Examining the justification for giving credence to personal testimony expands this movement and adds to it the plane of faith as well.

Felman and Laub (1992) see personal testimony as 'existential testimony', in which real pieces of life are delivered, and describe it as a tool for conveying an event, reality, position or dimension beyond the witness himself.

They note:

> Existential testimonies are not just evidences that concern private existence, but touching points between words and life, and they can be assimilated into us as pieces of real life.[51]

Sagi (2017) points to the similarity between this description of personal testimony as "Existential Testimonies" and the description of the testimony of a witness of faith.

He notes:

> The testimony of the witness of faith, allows what is beyond him to appear . . . Faith, in the deep senses, is a unique type of testimony, that restores the time of the occurrence for a person, and places it in the present.[52]

A link between belief in spoken personal testimony and belief in God has also appeared in literature. Kafka (2007), for example, wrote in one of the fragments:

> No man can live without perpetual trust in something indestructible in him, though the indestructible, as well as the trust in it, may always remain concealed from him. One of the possibilities of expression of this concealment is the belief in God.[53]

Another tier to this line of thought is raised by Sagi (2017),[54] arguing that the position of one who is ready to sacrifice his life for his faith is found in the base of the "Trust theory of testimony" by Faulkner (2007),[55] according to which the validity of testimony is based not on the certainty of the statements in the spoken testimony, but on trust in the emotional state of the person delivering his testimony. So, if we go one step further, a person's willingness to surrender his soul is, therefore, the basis for trusting his testimony.[56]

The position of the religious believer, by its very nature, does not need justifications. In Wittgenstein's language, it is "unshakable faith", meaning that it is a faith that is not reached 'inferentially' or by any other regular ways of validating a belief.[57]

The only way to convey the fullness of the experience of personal testimony is via the inner story. Thus, the principle underlying the belief in personal testimony is not anchored in the examination of the statements, which by their nature are refutable, but is based on the subject and his feelings, experiences and intentions; And similar to the position of the religious believer, its confirmation is existential.

The recipient's trust is a critical element in personal testimony. His/her trust is a necessary condition for its existence and on which the contributive qualities of testimony – such as gaining relief, receiving recognition, validating the occurrence, maintaining a continuum of life narrative and even self-establishment of the addressee – rely.

Without trust, all of these are not possible.

The Objective

"In the Absence of fearing it, testimony can be a relief"
"Essays in the First Person", **Appelfeld, Aharon** 1979[58]

The burden of spoken personal testimony, which is sometimes also given as legal testimony, such as in the Eichmann trial (1961–1962), is completely unique and is very lonely.

Paul Celan writes,

"No One
bears witness for the
witnesses."[59]

This line of Celan's poem argues for absolute responsibility and extreme loneliness and carries the great anguish that, in its loneliness, it echoes the burden of the testimony of Ishmael, the only survivor and the only witness to the shipwreck of Moby-Dick: "And I Only Am Escaped Alone To Tell Thee".[60]

Every person seeks a witness to his life and even to his death, not only in pain or disappointment but to a very wide range of experiences, from personal achievements, through personal or family secrets, to shameful deeds, which are heavy to contain alone.

Thus, from my point of view, and evidence for it is scattered throughout the book, the burden of the witness is indeed heavy, but the power of voiced testimony is in relieving the weight of the burden and in breaching the isolation of the testifier.

Haviva Pedaia challenges this claim and raises the question of, "What is the benefit of personal stimony?" Indeed, the advantage is not self-evident.

Pedaya tries to answer her own question in her book "*Stamps*" (2014):

Every personal testimony, concerning the weight of each story, may turn out to be unnecessary. And that may always be so if we expect stories to bring back something that has been lost. The ability of stories is limited. The stories will only give me a pause in time between expressing the impending disaster and realizing that the disaster has already occurred.

Is that not a lot?[61]

Martin Buber writes of a similar advantage (1948):

The matter of the story is more than mere speech, it actually transmits what happened to future generations; moreover, the act of the story itself is an event. . . .

One rabbi, was asked to tell a story. "A story", said the Rabbi, "should be told in such a way that it itself will be a salvation."[62]

The Special Status of Personal Testimony in the Field of Holocaust Research

Anyone who comes to investigate events during the Holocaust encounters the terrible difficulty of testifying about those events, in the problem of the paucity of documentary material and its lack of systematicity and continuity.

This missing is what Ida Fink calls 'emptiness', and refers to the concept of "deep memory", which was coined in the seminary of Holocaust researcher Lawrence Langer,[63] and is today one of the key concepts in postmodern historiography of the Holocaust.

In her book "*Peace of Time*" (1975),[64] Ida Fink talks about "The time that is not measured by month but by the word".[65] In her stories, which all of them touch the Holocaust, she presents another level of consciousness and another perception of time.

Ben Naftali Berkowitz (1993) describes a broad and universal phenomenon of 'a tractate of sharp silences' in relation to the Holocaust, in society and the philosophical world, which lasted about two decades after the end of the war and expressed emotional and rational helplessness.[66]

"The silence, or the paralysis, was of the individual and of society as a whole. Aahron Appelfeld called it "A coma of oblivion, the materials of memory, which are a sign of a past that refuses to disappear."[67]

This lack of narrative remains in the body as a broadcast that refuses translation and refuses to mediate between past and present. There is something that must be told, and that cannot be said – a void, a space hidden from the other, whose nature is the inability to be brought to light.

Much has been written about the physical symptom as language in the context of traumas. The obvious thing being that both the physical symptom and the social and philosophical silence express the inability to bear the meaning of the horror.

Personal testimonies of Jewish and non-Jewish witnesses, who have been there and saw, fill this void. Ullman (2006) refers to this:

> The witness who listens to the narrated testimony, allows the formation of the missing narrative. The witness makes the absence meaningful. Through spoken language the trauma becomes a loss, which is bounded in time and place and can be returned to, or taken ownership of it. While the absence represents the compulsive takeover of a mythical, boundless and unspeakable trauma.[68]

Spoken testimony places the trauma in an area of real-time, historically and geographically.

Primo Levi related to it in his book "*The Downed and the Saved*" (1986):

> Of course, the most substantial material for reconstructing the truth about the camps is the survivors' memories . . . Today, many years later, we can safely say

that the story of the Lagers has been written almost exclusively by people who, like me . . . did not plumb the depths. The ones who did, never returned, or if they did, their capacity for observation was paralyzed by pain and incomprehension.[69]

In practice, Holocaust research brings together those who give testimony and its researchers around the tension between the objective and the subjective and between the private and the public experience. In doing so, 'public' testimonies were also of great importance, given mainly out of a sense of duty and of a national mission.

Spoken testimony delivered in public is not similar to a testimony given in a private setting. Lubin recognized the difference between the private and the public when, in an article (1999), she wrote about the witness Zvia Lubetkin, who, before testifying in public, testified privately in a closed and private room.

Orly Lubin noted:

The two testimonies, the first of which we will never know. That testimony is an expression of the truth. The tears brought about by the first testimony have not yet been wiped away. The room, the grove, the path in Beit Oren, become a transit site. A transitional that precedes the testimony, which is a private speech about herself, about her most horrific privacy – to the public moment in which the intimate is exposed to criticism – in order to function as part of the estab-lishment of the self-image of the pioneering movement. The second testimony was not in conformity with the processes of testimony as laid out by Dori Laub (1992), Shaul Friedlander (1992), James Young (1993), or Lawrence Langer (1995), to create catharsis, or work of mourning, or representation. Its purpose was to make evidence available to the movement.[70]

The Power of Personal Testimony in Cultural-Social Change

The arena examined here is the Jewish settlement in Eretz, Israel, after World War II until the mid-1990s of the 20th century.

In the 1950s of the last century, a social dichotomy was created in Israel between the veterans of the Jewish settlement and the immigrants from Eastern Europe. The social institutions reinforced a collective consensus of a "negation of the exile".

Researchers of society in Israel have addressed this phenomenon. Anita Shapira (1977) noted that immigrants, who for a time were considered foreigners, were a positive factor in tightening a Zionist identity.[71] Moshe Zuckerman (2001) wrote in a similar vein that the state did not confront the reality of the immigrant as a subject, and there was an 'objectification' of the new immigrant so as to justify the Zionist ideology.[72]

Even more serious were the views of Yechiam Weitz (1990), who spoke of a process of de-legitimization of the immigrant in the 1950s, and Nurit Gretz (1999), who wrote, "Zionism, which built the Hebrew-Israeli identity, on the denial of the

Jewish Diaspora, always needed the identity of the exiled Jew to define itself, by way of contrast."[73]

Most of the immigrants remained foreigners, in their own country, for many years.

In his book *"What Makes a Society Possible"* (1910),[74] Georg Zimmel points to the foreignness of immigrants:

> The reference to stranger is to one who comes today and stays tomorrow [. . .] His status within the group is determined precisely because he did not belong to it in the first place, and therefore brings to it qualities that do not derive from it. [. . .] An element whose immanent status simultaneously involves being outside and facing it." In the intimate relationship between a person and a person, the foreigner can be attractive and make significant contributions, but as long as he is considered a stranger, in the eyes of others he is not a 'landowner'. Another expression is the objectivity of the stranger – he is not essentially committed to the group's one-sided tendencies.[75]

The lack of recognition of the personal story of immigrants and the abilities of their enormous contribution to the state and society left them closed in their communities; in addition, their different opinions established them as enemies.

Axel Honneth analyzed at length the invisibility phenomenon and pointed out two meanings of it: the perceptual standard meaning, whereby the object is entirely invisible and is not physically present, and the meaning that is important in the present context, which Honneth calls 'metaphorical invisibility', that is, non-existence in a social sense.[76]

Honneth traces the history of the culture in which "the dominant expresses their social superiority by not perceiving those they dominate."[77] The invisibility of servants, of blacks and of various other "transparent" elements, is not a result of optical barriers; as physical entities, they are visible, but their invisibility reflects the negation of their identity as "persons with clearly defined properties."[78]

Honneth adds that recognition is recognition of subjectivity and not only in the location in the field of vision . . . the need for recognition is a need for extensive recognition – recognition of the person's qualities, ideas, values, ideals, achievements and all these is based on attention, on listening and not on seeing. That is, what is needed to provide recognition is not the nod but the listening.

And indeed, listening to the immigrants' testimonies did change their social status. Israel of the 1950s was a land that was obliged to forget! The collective consensus created a consciousness of non-recognition of exile, and its main tool was culture. This is how a 'social anomaly' was created.

According to Mary Douglas (1966), every culture must deal with a 'social anomaly'; she lists five ways of dealing with such a phenomenon, one of which is to perform rituals combining ambiguous symbols in order to expand their meaning, such as combining poetry and mythology. These "facilitate combining evil and death with life and the good and create from them a uniform and unifying pattern."[79]

Giving testimony by voice, especially testimony given in public with a committee, is certainly a ritual.[80]

Three Periods of the Discourse on Testimony in Israel

Danny Gutwein (2009) divided the process of building the collective memory of the Holocaust in Israel into three periods.[81] These are also the three phases in the status and cultural-social influence of the testimonial discourse of the community in Israel.

The first period – which Gutwein terms "split reaction". It begins with the Eichmann trial (1961/1962), in which the value of the survivors' testimonies was recognized historically and legally. The status of the discourse of testimony increased, but its social impact remained limited.

The second period – is called 'nationalized memory' and lasted from the mid-1970s to the mid-1980s. During this period, much appreciation was given to testimonies given in public, most of them out of a sense of mission, mainly due to their contribution to national/collective and shared memory.

The status of private testimony was not yet considered at this time, but it was a leading stage.

The third period – was the period of 'privatized memory', which began in the mid-1980s after the release of the film "Holocaust", which, as mentioned, became a founding event in the discourse of testimony in the Western world. During this period, attention was paid in Israel to the personal experiences of the immigrants and marked the rise of the social and value status of the individual testimony.

The beneficial influence of personal testimony is based on two conditions: the willingness to listen and the desire to tell.

Both existed during this time phase: social institutions encouraged a multiplicity of personal testimonies, and these formed a bridge between past and present and between immigrants and natives in Israel. Listening to life stories dismantled the group of immigrants into individuals, which made them be seen as less different, less threatening and closer light.

Especially relevant here is what Axel Honneth (1949) pointed out about the critical role of language and speech in integrating immigrants into society:

Speech is an expression of the subjective world of the individual and he who needs recognition. Giving recognition takes place in three circles, from the immediate circle of a family, to wider social circles and is based on listening and not just on sight.[82]

The stories of the immigrants began to be a part of the school curriculum, which made them a part of the national consensus. The narrative of the stories, or films and plays about immigrants, changed.

Nurit Gretz (1999) related to this issue and wrote about the dismantling of the Zionist narrative: "The link that dominated until then between the gender and the nation that appeared in the literature, cinema and theater, of the Jewish as feminine and the Israeli as the masculine, – was rejected and didn't return."[83]

A by-product of this, which seems unintentional: an analogy has been created between the enemy that arose to destroy the Jewish people and the Arab enemy, an analogy which creates an ultimate unification in the face of a common enemy.

A Number of Comments in Concluding Part 1

This part of the book is like a business card to the phenomenon of spoken testimony. The narrative of the phenomenon is fascinating.

Spoken testimony is a daily phenomenon. It is with us all the time, its visibility is confusing and the need for it is only felt when it is absent. The act of testimony has undergone a paradigmatic shift from being a one-dimensional act that provides information to a multidimensional act recognized as a medium of healing.

The roots of the turning point were planted in the traumas of World War II, but the change has only become evident during the last decade of the 20th century when the philosophical and cultural-social backgrounds were prepared for changes in concepts. The Eichmann trial (1961–1962) and the film "Holocaust" (1985) by Claude Lantzman were significant milestones in changing the status of the discourse of testimony.

The three types of testimony – legal, natural and personal – have been explored here in detail, but the book's main interest is the personal testimony and from now on, the reference is to it only.

Spoken testimony has no theoretical anchor. It seems to be more of a concern of an action than of a theory. The discussion places it and the problems rooted in it in the space between two respected philosophical questions: the question of 'certainty' and the question of the 'other'.

An analysis of the phenomenon of testimony, its meanings and components in philosophical and linguistic tools in this part of the book prepares the ground for the psychoanalytic discussion in Part 2. The rationale underlying this structure is based on the assumption that there is a direct connection between philosophical thinking and psychoanalytic practice, and the best way to analyze psychoanalytic issues is via philosophy.

List of References and Notes

1 This is how the Bible is called in Hebrew.
2 Tractate of testimonies is repeated on the day that Rabbi Elazar Ben Azariah was placed in charge and the guard of the entrance at the Beit Midrash was dismissed. All the sages

entered, each testifying what he heard from his rabbis, and there was no halakha that was subject to doubt that he did not interpret (Brachot 28).

3   Mamonides, Mishneh-Tora. *The Book of Judges* (Jerusalem: Halakhot Edut, Koren Publishing). Laws of Testimonies, pp. 18–22. Moses ben Maimon (1138–1204), known as Maimonides (Rambam in Hebrew – רמב״ם), the author of "Mishneh Torah" in which he composed a code of Jewish law with the widest-possible scope and depth. The work gathers all the binding laws from the Talmud and the Mishna.

4   Ibid., "Sefer Hamitzvot", "to do", p. 178. "The duty to give a true testimony".

5   Ibid., p. 179.

6   Ibid.

7   Drori Moshe (2004): "Da'at: Herzog College for Jewish and Spiritual Studies". *Parashat Leviticus*, 20.

8   "Sefer Hamizvot", "Don't do", p. 297.

9   Maimonides, "Shulchan-Aruch", verse 28:1.

10 Ibid.

11 This discussion is based on the article by Rafael, Yaakobi, 2004, "Da'at", "Remedies Following False Testimony", "Parshat Nitzavim", 90.

12 Raphael Yaakobi comments that there are those who joked that if the prohibitions in the Ten Commandments were recorded in the community records or written in a customary doctrine that is practiced, everyone would be much more careful about them than they are when they are written in the Ten Commandments.

13 This discussion is based on Eldad Perry's article, "Between Factual Truth and Legal Truth – the Hidden and the Revealed", "*Da'at*", "*Parashat Nitzavim*": – *Vayelech*, 2003, Issue No. 138.

14 Verdict by the High Court of Justice 152/82. Daniel Elon against the government of Israel. Verdict: 36 (4) 449, pp. 466–467.

15 Elon (2001), p. 278: "Legal truth and factual truth", withholding information from court for the sake of protecting social values. "Legal Studies", 24 (2001), p. 263.

16' Raphael Yacakoby in Da'at (2005): "An Immediate Impression of Evidence and Alternatives". Parashat Noach Genesis, Chapter 6, p. 182.

17 "Talmudic Encyclopedia. Volume 1 "A witness cannot become a Judge".

18 Mishne Tora – Sefer Hamitzvot – Digest Negative commandment.

19 The Maimonides, "Basic laws of the Tora", ch. 8, halakha 2.

20 The Mishnayot of the Maimonides chapter 7, Mishna 3.

21 There is a controversy here. The Gemara relates: Rabbi Abba sat and stated this *halakha* that a witness can become a judge. Rav Safra raised an objection to the opinion of Rabbi Abba from a mishna (*Rosh HaShana* 25b). If three people saw the new moon and they constitute a court, two of them should stand and seat two of their colleagues to sit near the remaining individual judge. And the two should testify before the three judges, and they should then recite the standard formula for sanctifying the month: sanctified is the month, sanctified. Two others must join the original judge to form a tribunal of three judges, as an individual judge is not deemed credible to sanctify the month by himself. And if it enters your mind to say that "A witness can become a judge, why do I need all this?" Let the three judges remain seated in their place and sanctify the month, as they can be both witnesses and judges.

22 Aquinas, Thomas (1250): *Commentary on Boethinus's De Trinitate*.

23 Coady, Cecil Anthony John (1992), *Testimony: A Philosophical Study*. Clarendon Press, Oxford, pp. 56–57.

24 Kedmi, Yaakov (2006): *On Evidence*. Part three and part four. Chapters on testimony. Publishing Law Books, Tel Aviv, Israel (Hebrew).

25 Felman, Shoshana and Laub, Dori (1992): *Crises of Witnessing in Literature, Psychoanalysis and History*. Routledge, Great Britan; Taylor and Francis, New York, p. 117

26 Paul Celan, W. W. (2000): *Selected Poems and Prose*. Norton & Co. Inc. New York City, NY.
27 Amir, Dana (2013): *Cleft Tongue, The Inner Me*. Magnes Publishing, Jerusalem, Israel. Chapter 5: "The Inner Witness", p. 1 (Hebrew).
28 Ibid., pp. 5–6.
29 Quoted by Dori Laub (2005), in his article "Traumatic Shutdown of Narrative and Symbolization, A Death Instinct Derivative?" *Contemporary Psychoanalysis*, 41: 307–326. Published Online: 23 Oct 2013.
30 Sándor Ferenczi, M. D. (1988): "Confusion of Tongues between Adults and the Child: The Language of Tenderness and of Passion". *Contemporary Psychoanalysis*, 24, pp. 196–206.
31 Balint, Michael (1933): *The Basic Fault: Therapeutic Aspects of Regression*. Northwestern University Press, Evanston, IL (1969).
32 Ferenczi, Sándor (1933): *The Clinical Diary of Sándor Ferenczi*, ed. Judith Dupont, trans. Michael Balint. Harvard University Press, Cambridge, MA (1995).
33 Felman, Shoshana and Laub, Dori (1992): *Crises of Witnessing in Literature, Psychoanalysis and History*. Routledge, Great Britan; Taylor and Francis, New York, p. 93.
34 Sagi, Avi (2009): *The Voyage to Meaning, A Philosophical-Hermeneutical Study of Literary Works*. Bar Ilan University Press, Ramat Gan, Israel, pp. 152–156 (Hebrew).
35 Levi, Primo (2015): *The Complete Works of Primo Levi*. Liveright, New York City, New York, pp. 2419–2420. ISBN 13: 9780871404565.
36 Sagi, Avi (2009), p. 159 (Hebrew).
37 Felman and Laub (1992), p. 109.
38 Ibid.
39 Sagi, Avi (2009), p. 159 (Hebrew).
40 It is appropriate here to add the contribution of the imagination in the establishment of the real occurrence in a verbal event.
41 Buber, Martin (1969): *The Hidden Light* (1979). Shoken Publishing House Ltd, Tel Aviv, Israel, p. 7 (Hebrew).
42 Heidegger (1978): *Heidegger and Modern Philosophy: Critical Essays*. Yale University Press, New Haven, p. 59.
43 Ibid., pp. 193–194.
44 Ibid.
45 Celan, Paul (1959): *Collected Poetry and Prose*, Translated by Shimon Sandbank, Hakibbutz Hameuchad, Bnei Brak, Israel, p. 169 (1994) (Hebrew).
46 Felman and Laub (1992), pp. 37–38.
47 Celan (1959), p. 169 (Hebrew).
48 Ibid.
49 Amichai, Yehuda (2016): Zwizchen Kreig und Liebe, Der Dichter Jeuda Amichai. "My Judaism". Translated by: Hanna Livnat. Rimonim Publishing, Giv`atayim, Israel, p. 21 (Hebrew).
50 Felman and Laub (1992), p. 70.
51 Ibid., p. 21
52 Sagi, Avi (Ed.) (2017): *In the Beginning Is Believer*. Carmel Publishing House, Collaborators: Shalom Hartman Institute, Jerusalem, Israel, p. 22 (Hebrew).
53 Kafka, Franz (1998): Die acht Octavhefte. Translatd by Shimon Zandbenk Am Oved Publishers Ltd. Tel Aviv, Israel: Die acht Oktavhefte. Am Oved Publishers Ltd. Tel Aviv, Israel, *Fragments*, p. 52 (Hebrew).
54 Sagi, Avi (2017), p. 38 (Hebrew).
55 Faulkner (2007), pp. 95–101. In this context, one has also to refer to Tess Dewhurst who developed the theory and whose concepts were detailed in the earlier discussion of trust in testimony.

56 Most relevant to this matter is also Therese Dewhurst's thesis: "Take My Word for It: A New Approach to the Problem of Sincerity in the Epistemology of Testimony", *Rhodes University*. United States (2010).

57 Wittgenstein, Ludwig (1967): *Lectures and Conversations on Aesthetics and Psychology*. Blackwell Publishing, London, England, p. 54.

58 Appelfeld, Aharon (1979): *Essays in the First Person. ""The Horror and the Commitment"*. The Zionist Library, The World Zionist Organization, Jerusalem, Israel (Hebrew).

59 Celan, Paul (1968): *Ash-Glory*, trans. Pierre Joris. Poetry Foundation Publishing, Chicago, IL.

60 Herman, Melville (1922): *Moby-Dick; or The Whale*. C. H. Simonds Company, Boston, MA. Epilog, p. 533.

61 Pdaia, Haviva (2014): *Stamps*. Yedioth Sfarim Publishing, Rishon Lezion, Israel (Hebrew).

62 Martin, Buber (1948): *The Hidden Light* (1979). Shoken Publishing House Ltd, Tel Aviv, Israel, p. 7 (Hebrew).

63 Lawrence Langer distinguishes between two types of memory. One, 'deep memory' – an eruption of past memory into the present. All memory is concentrated in the Holocaust and there is an identification of the 'I' as if no time has passed. The second is a 'shared memory' – which has boundaries between past and present, and there is a possibility to look at the past through the present, and there is no assimilation into the 'I' of the 'Shoah'.

64 Fink, Ida (1975): *Peace of Time*, trans. Nachman Ben Ami. Masada Publishing, Ramat-Gan, Israrel (Hebrew).

65 In a short story within the book called "*A Piece of Time*", Ida Fink writes that she always wanted to recall a piece of time that is not measured in months but in words, but she had no strength. She feared that this time (i.e. her life after the Holocaust) could destroy her memories that were at the time not measured in months.

66 Ben Naftali, Michal Berwkowitz (1993): "The Israeli Philosophers and the Holocaust". *Theory and Criticism*, 4, 1993, pp. 57–78 (Hebrew).

67 Appelfeld, Aharon (1999): *The Story of a Life*. Shoken Publications House, Tel Aviv, Israel, p. 6 (Hebrew).

68 Ullman, Chana (2006): "Bearing Witness: Across the Barriers in Society and in the Clinic". *Psychoanalytic Dialogs* 16, pp. 181–198.

69 Levi, Primo (2015): *The Complete Works of Primo Levi*. Liveright, New York City, NY, p. 2416.

70 Lubin, Orli (1999): "The Truth Between the Frames of the Truth: Autobiography, Testimony, Body and Site". In: *Aderet Lebinyamin: The Jubilee Book of Binyamin Hershav*, Hakibutz Hameuhad Publising House, Bnei Brak, Israel, Vol. 1, 1999 (Hebrew).

71 Shapira, Anita (1977). *Hama'avak Hanichzav* (The Futile Struggle). Am Oved Publishing House, Tel Aviv, Israel (Hebrew).

72 Zuckerman, Moshe (2001). *The Israeli Mill: Myth a in a Conflicted Society*. Resling, Tel Aviv, Israel (2001).

73 Nurit Gretz in "Aderet LeBinyamin (1999)": The Jubilee Book of Binyamin Hershav. *Literature Meaning Culture: Porter's Israeli Institute of Poetics and Semiotics*. Hakibbutz Hameuhad Publishing House, Bnei Brak, Israel (Hebrew).

74 Georg, Z. Simmel (1910): "*What Makes a Society Possible?*" and Other Essays by Georg Simmel. Hakibuts Hmeuhad Publishing House, Bnei Brak, Israel (2012) (Hebrew).

75 Ibid., p. 254.

76 Honneth, Axel (2001) in – Sagi, Avi (2012): "*Living with the Other*": *Contributions to Phenomenology*. Springer International Publishing, Cham, Switzerland (2019), p. 102.

77 Honneth, Axel (2001). "Invisibility: On the Possibility of 'Recognition'". *Proceedings of the Aristotelian Society, Supplementary*. Oxford University Press, Oxford, England 75, pp. 111–139.

78 Ibid.
79 Douglas, Mari (1966): *Purity and Danger: An Analysis of Concepts of Pollution and Taboo*. Routledge, Abingdon, UK.
80 Research by Inger Agger and Soren Jensen (1990) emphasize the universality of spoken testimony as an act of ceremonial healing.
81 Gutwein, Danny (2009), Criticism of the 'negation of the Diaspora' and the privatization of Israeli consciousness. Published in *"The Jews in the Present"* – gathering and dispersal; Editors: Eliezer Ben-Raphael [and others]. Yad Yitzhak Ben-Zvi, Jerusalem, pp. 7–52 (Hebrew).
82 Honneth, Axel (2001), p. 52 (Hebrew).
83 Gretz, Nurit (1999), p. 68 (Hebrew).

Part 2

Testimony as a Therapeutic Function in Psychoanalysis and Psychotherapy

Chapter 6

Everyone Wants His Voice to Be Heard

Zipi Rosenberg Schipper

He

"I want to tell you my life."

We met every week.

He was always punctual and always paid in cash.

I only knew his first name.

Expressionless face, buttoned-up shirt, brown shoes.

Not especially tall, but when he entered, the room filled up.

"I want to tell you my life", he said immediately as he sat down.

A moment later, he added: "But I don't want you to interrupt me. That bothers me.

"Do you agree?"

We both remained silent.

While I was thinking that nothing in my studies of psychology had prepared me for such an opening, I replied.

"Yes, I agree."

This was the beginning of a unique therapeutic alliance that taught me the power of testimony.

We met once a week for nearly two years.

He always chose to sit on the solid chair rather than the soft couch.

"I'm not good at small talk", he said apologetically and began to tell his story the moment he entered.

He spoke monotonously, his gaze pensive and fastened on one spot. Only occasionally did his voice become hoarse, as if flooded by uncontrollable emotions.

At the beginning, he feared that he wouldn't convey things well and kept to a strictly chronological order in telling his story. Sometimes, the memory rebelled, refusing to cooperate. As time passed, he became more confident, and his speech became more associative, as in recollection, in which events are raised regardless of the time in which they occurred.

"This is my real life", he said; "what for others is of no interest is for me the whole world.

"Thank you for listening to me."

DOI: 10.4324/9781003403920-8

He spoke at length, with a sense of longing. He went into details. At times, he spoke fluently; then, at times, he was lost for words. He spread out pieces of life that encompassed both beauty and pain, the torment of parting and the hardships of wanderings, together with a good life and youthful loves and a sporting excellence.

When he spoke, he plunged in body and mind, delving into the stories, and I listened in absolute silence.

At the end of the hour, he suddenly became aware of time and place, and as the way he started the session, so he ended it – in a cut.

And me, what was I there throughout the meetings?
I was a witness to his story.

As time went by, I discovered in myself an ability for a different kind of listening. I was amazed by how profound listening can be when subjectivity moves aside, when there is no need to prove something, to find a wise interpretation, or to search for an appropriate response. Just to be, to be present.

And then came the last meeting.
"That's it", he said, "I've reached the 'now', and this is our last meeting."

This time he told me how he had lived as a stranger in his home. Although ostensibly he had adapted well, the sense of foreignness hadn't left him. In fact, he had never lost interest in that life across the sea, and he tried in every way to capture the interest of his immediate family, his wife, his children, to tell them the story of his 'previous life' but was constantly rebuffed and treated with contempt. Also, the trophies he had won as a sportsman, which had once been prominently displayed on a stylish cabinet, had been tossed into a closed drawer.

His chances of finding an ideal listener were slim. He also knew that in the absence of a listener, the story was liable to collapse. The memories began to fade until he himself started to doubt their actual existence. But he couldn't come to terms with the story disappearing as if it had never happened.

He was clinging to his memories.

When fragments of memories gained control of his daily life, a sense of urgency to tell his story began to burn inside him, as Aharon Appelfeld wrote in his book "*The Story of a Life*" (2006): "The delicate emotions stand naked. The need to clothe the memories in words becomes stronger and stronger."[1]

When he got up to go, he thanked me for the room that was isolated from every other reality and that no one, but us, knows or will know what had been said in it and how important it is for him to have a witness to his life.

We then both stood up.
He said, "You helped me a lot."
He shook my hand warmly in a way I hadn't known before.
We were both silent.

Can I ask a question?
"Yes", he answered
Of all that was here, what helped you?
"I saw that you cared."
His sealed, expressionless face had changed.

Everyone Wants Their Voice to Be Heard

A person's voice has many meanings. On occasion, it expresses his wish, sometimes his feelings or his desires and sometimes his past. In this case, deep listening to his voice sustains his past.

This is a very personal story, yet, at the same time, it is universal and raises existential difficulty in the sense of a loss of continuity in the life of migrants across the globe.

Yehudah Amichai, who was an immigrant, wrote, "Whoever experienced migration and is between here and there, senses his identity as a rupture and a crisis".[2]

The act of testimony creates a space of attention to the missing story and contains the memories and experiences from the past. It has a vitally important role in psychic healing, in safeguarding the sense of life's continuity, in the establishment of the self, in the release of emotions, in easing a time of distress and in perpetuating a person's inner experience.

List of References and Notes

1 Appelfeld, Aharon (2006): *The Story of a Life*. Shocken Publications House, Tel Aviv Israel (Hebrew).
2 Yehuda, Amichai (2016): *Zwizchen Kreig und Liebe: Der Dichter (Between War and Love)* (Renate Eichmeir und Edith Raim). Printed, by Rimonim-Publishing, Giv'atayim Israel, p. 33 (Hebrew).

Chapter 7

The Roles of Personal Testimony and Witnessing in Our Lives

Zipi Rosenberg Schipper

Introduction

The range of roles, or more correctly, the contributions of personal testimony and witnessing in a person's life, is wide and difficult to fully realize. Sometimes the need for testimony is visible and observable and sometimes covert, but it always exists.

The focus of this chapter is on the universal psychological aspects of personal testimony. The presentation is random, there is no hierarchy because the importance of the roles of the testimony varies from person to person.

Some of the main contributions of testimony and witnessing in our life elaborated here relief, recognition, validity, maintaining a sense of continuity in a person's life, vital role in developmental stage and eternalizing a life story.

The discussions on the roles of testimony detailed here, are a call for attention to the significant aspects of testimony. Some of them were mentioned in previous discussions in the book, therefore the discussions about them are relatively brief.

Let us delve into these roles of spoken personal testimony.

Personal Testimony Is a Relief

> *"Anxiety weighs down the heart, and a kind word cheers it up."*
>
> (Proverbs 25:12)

The element of relief of emotional heaviness, or alleviation of loneliness, which can result from physical pain, a failure or a difficult experience, as well as from feeling lonely with an experience of personal success that is unknown to those immediately surrounding that person, goes all the way back to the Bible. Everyone is familiar with the easing and comforting effect that results from talking in front of a caring witness about pain or an unrecognized achievement. Every child knows that it is not worth crying if his mother, father, caretaker, or any significant other is not around. As in Yehuda Atlas's Hebrew poem *"And This Child is Me"*:

DOI: 10.4324/9781003403920-9

Far from home
I was beaten
By a big child-
On the way home the weeping lessened
I saw my mother
And it started again.
Yehuda Atlas (1977)[1]

This aspect of alleviating emotional pain through listening and paying attention to the other's testimony is a well-known tool in ancient therapeutic wisdom, like going to a shaman, a rabbi or a priest. An issue that is found a great deal in literature, poetry or art.

In one of the interviews given by Primo Levi, he talks about the need for emotional relief through a spoken testimony:

> I remember *very* clearly certain train journeys in 1945, just after my return, travelling around Italy to salvage, to put back together, my work prospects. I was looking for a job. And on the train, I remember telling my stories to whoever I found myself with . . . If you ask me why I wanted to tell the stories, I couldn't answer. Probably it was part of an understandable instinct: I wanted to free myself from them . . . I like to tell people my stories. And indeed, I do tell them, mostly stories that have really happened to me or ones that have been told to me by others. Telling them and retelling them I feel as though I am in line with a millennial dynasty that goes back all the way to the popular storytellers of Africa and Asia. If you ask me why, I'll suggest you talk to a psychoanalyst, because I am not very expert in the roots of being human.[2]

The Role of Testimony in Maintaining Life's Continuity

The importance of testimony in preserving the sense of continuity in life is most evident among three populations:

- Immigrants.
- People who had been captives, especially long-term prisoners.
- People who suffer from psychotic attacks or temporary loss of consciousness.

Common to all three is the interruption in the continuity of life, which creates a gulf between what had been before the event and what happened thereafter.

The therapeutic story that appears in the prologue sheds light on the implications of a loss of a sense of continuity in life.

Silencing a person's memories harms the continuity of psychic life and influences the individual's day-to-day functioning and sense of social and familial belongingness.

The absence of a listening recipient may cause the memories to become clouded, and the person can no longer be sure whether they are real or whether he was imagining them, which can cause an undermining of the psyche.

This phenomenon is all the more valid in Israel, where immigrants are invited to erase their past. Sometimes, as in the described therapeutic story, despite a seemingly good adaptation, the silencing of such a significant part of a person's life caused a sense of foreignness to become rooted within him, and the basic experience of his existence in Israel becomes linked to an experience of non-belongingness and alienation.

In a similar yet slightly different way, people who experience psychotic episodes, states of regression, a temporary loss of consciousness or prolonged hospitalization due to serious physical or psychical illness, lose a part of their life's continuity and are critically in need of witnesses to fill the resulting lacuna.

Spoken testimony has a vital role in bridging the gap created there, because it has the power to construct the space of attention needed for the acquisition and inclusion of the missing story.

The Vital Role of Witnessing in the Developmental Stage

"The need for a witness is a vital human need, specifically, in developmental terms and the absence is a painfully lonely state."[3]

Seiden, Henry (1996)

The presence of a witness in a person's life is a significant condition of the integration of the self at every stage of life, but most especially important at the developmental stage. It can even be said that a child's normal development requires witnesses in his life. It won't be unreasonable to say that a child can know that he is experiencing a difficult reality in his life only if a witness observing him serves him as a mirror.

Seiden (1996) notes:

The absence (of a witness ZR) is a painfully lonely state which threatens the cohesion of self . . . We need the sense that our experience is shared in order to feel that our reasoning is firm, that what we know to be true is true, that what we feel is valid. This is so, of course, even in terms of identity and self-definition – it is the confirming presence of others which allows us to go on believing that we are who we think we are.[4]

Giving Recognition

Listening to what the other says gives him recognition. Axel Honneth (1931) teaches us what real recognition is; he notes: "What recognition requires is not identification but attention."[5]

Honneth emphasizes the significance of talking and listening in offering recognition and contends that the absence of fully recognizing a person leads him to feel fearful, angry, ashamed and bitter.

> Language and speech have a critical role to play when it comes to the issue of recognition . . . Giving recognition is not the knowledge of there being someone in view. It is a question of recognizing him . . . Recognition of a person is to recognize the entirety of his subjectivity in his inner world. . . . Therefore, what is required is not identification but rather being attentive, listening to him.[6]

Validation

A testimony that remains untold is kept in a person's inner world, in his own mind. It is validated when the concealed story moves from the private sphere and reaches an interpersonal space. The emotional experience turns into a channel of words and thereby moves from the field of consciousness to the physical arena. The witness to whom the words are communicated by virtue of him being a witness, as Orange noted, "witnessing is part of validation."[7] Orange adds that the witness has the power and the ability to give a name to what is being said, and giving a name to an event gives it validity, and so it acquires existence.

The experience of witnessing described in the prologue is, therefore, a recognition of the person's wholeness and a validation of his life story, which, over the years, had been clouded by the mist of uncertainty and pain, distance and forgetfulness.

The Element of Eternalization in Spoken Testimony

In the poem "For Man Thou Art and unto Man Shalt Thou Return" (Genesis 3:19), Yehuda Amichai asserts:

> *Between things dying and things that are living*
> *Is there a place, . . .*
> *For seeing, being seen? . . .*
> *Only lots of witnesses, lots of testimonies.*[8]
> > Yehuda Amichi (1998)

> *Deeds which populate the dimensions of space and which reach their end when someone dies may cause us wonderment. One thing, or an infinite number of things indeed die, unless there is a collective memory, as the Theosophists believe. What will die with me when I die, what pathetic or fragile form will the world lose?*[9]
> > **Jorge Borges**, *Labyrinths* (1957)

Occasionally, people deposit their testimony in the hands of others and ask them to save it for posterity. The publication of such stories could have fateful implications, mainly within the close family. The decision to bring these stories into the world derives mainly from the desire for relief or from the hardship of containing the burden alone, but mostly because of the fear that they will be lost forever, or as one said: "The secret is too important as to take it with me to the grave."

In addition, there is the hope that telling the story will lead to some kind of reparation. A moving example of the power of testimony in perpetuating a story and its reparation appears in S.Y. Agnon's story, "*And the crooked shall be made straight*" S.Y. Agnon (1931).[10]

In his introduction to the story, which he dedicated to his mother, Agnon writes:

> This is the tale of a man named Menashe Chaim, who lived in the holy community of Buczacz (may his city be rebuilt, amen) and fell upon hard times, losing everything he owned. . . . he was scorned and hounded but refrained from ruining the lives of others and so preserved his name and left behind a lasting legacy.[11]

In the final part of the story, after drifting for a long time, Menashe Chaim returns to his hometown. On the day of his arrival, he realizes that he is thought to be dead. His wife had married someone else, and they had a baby. Menashe Chaim knows he must disappear, or the baby will be considered a bastard. Tired and sore, he wishes to die.

Having nowhere else, he goes to the cemetery. There he sees his wife crying on a grave with a large and beautiful tombstone and his name engraved on it. The cemetery's guard sees his distress and gives him some food and drink and stays by his side. And after a while, he approached him and said, "As God lives and as my soul lives, your sufferings have touched my heart."[12] Menashe Chaim saw that he was filled with grief, and he knew that his woe had touched him, and he could no longer hold back.

And he said, "I will reveal today what I have not revealed to anyone, but once I will ask – that he not tell anyone anything of what I will tell him."

And then Menashe Haim tells the keeper of the graves that they were childless, and when he lost his possessions, he followed his wife's advice and wandered in the villages.

Before he left, he took a letter of recommendation from the Rebbe. And managed to collect a little money, and later a beggar chanced upon him on the road and tempted him to sell him the recommendation. When he returned home, he heard that he was counted among the dead and that his wife married another man, and they had a child. He didn't say, but it's clear that he must stay in his wanderings lest he consider this son a bastard".

It was clear to the keeper of the graves who he was, and after Menashe Haim passed away, the keeper buried him and put the beautiful tombstone on his grave. The tombstone that bears his name and was mistakenly over the beggar's grave.

And so, by the right of the delivery of his testimony, Menashe Haim "preserved his name and gained a lasting legacy".

List of References and Notes

1 Atlas, Yehuda (1977): *And This Child Is Me*. Keter Publishing House Ltd., Jerusalem, Israel (Hebrew).
2 Levi, Primo (2015): *The Voice of Memory*. Wiley, Hoboken, New Jersey, USA, Kindle Edition, pp. 3186–3194.
3 Seiden, H. (1996): "The Healing Presence. Part 1: The Witness as Self-Object Function". *Psychoanalytic Review*, 83, pp. 685–693, p. 690.
4 Ibid., p. 687.
5 Honneth, Axel (2001): "Invisibility: On the Possibility of 'Recognition'". *Proceedings of the Aristotelian Society, Supplementary*. Oxford University Press, Oxford, 75, pp. 111–139, 51.
6 Ibid., p. 69.
7 Orange, Donna M. (1996): *Emotional Understanding: Studies in Psychoanalytic Epistemology*, The Guilford Press, New York and London (1995), p. 137.
8 Amichai, Yehuda (1998): *For Man Thou Art and unto Man Shalt Thou Return*. Shocken Publishing House Ltd, Tel Aviv, Israel, p. 47.
9 Borges, Jorge Luis (1960): *Labyrinths*. Keter Publishing, Bnei Brak, Israel (1986), p. 151 (Hebrew).
10 Agnon, Shmuel Yosef (1933): "And the Crooked Shall Be Made Straight". In: *Of Such and of Such*. Toby Press, New Milford, CT (1996).
11 Ibid., p. 103.
12 Ibid., p. 105.

Chapter 8

The Function of Testimony in Psychoanalysis and Psychotherapy

Zipi Rosenberg Schipper

Introduction

"To make sense of things, . . . to bring order, reality, and value requires the responsible presence of others. . . . To refer to this presence as bearing witness allows us to draw on ancient wisdom in understanding what such presence means – and to see psychoanalytic work in the context of centuries-old cultural experience."[1]

Henry, M. Seiden (1996)

In the therapeutic context, analysts do not commonly use the concept of 'testimony'. This is mainly because the concept is considered to be related to the legal field or historical documentation. In Wittgenstein's formulation, it belongs to a different "language-game" (sprachspiel). This misses out on an important function that is indeed accepted in other discourses but is also of significance in the clinical field.

The psychological aspects of the act of testimony are identified in the writings of researchers such as Miller (1991), Herman (1992), Feldman & Laub (2008), Seiden (1996), Goffman (1997), Poland (2000); Orange (1996), Ullman (2006), Aron (2013) and others as a -- significant transformative experience that, at its core, signifies the attainment of recognition, the establishment of self, validates the reality of the subject and easing distress – justifies examining the importance of the concept in the psychoanalytic language game.

It should be noted that the first to write about the therapeutic value of testimony were the mental health teams who worked with the victims of an oppressive military regime in Chile. In articles they published in the 1970s, the researchers describe an improvement in symptoms of post-traumatic distress suffered by witnesses, once they had delivered their testimony. This, when compared to their considerable distress during their questioning about the same events in a prior investigation that had taken place in differing circumstances and for another purpose.

The act of testimony in therapy is a new concept in the professional lexicon. To date, no philosophical, psychological or societal theory has bestowed its authority upon it. Thus, from many points of view, the progression and its rootedness in the psychoanalytic field evoke a philosophical model of thought that develops from its

DOI: 10.4324/9781003403920-10

own internal necessity and, in the course of its development, bundles theoretical thought with clinical experience.[2]

The sources of personal testimony are linked to the field of religious belief, and it reached the therapeutic field already charged with the connotations from there.

The act of testimony itself gains no attention in psychoanalytic epistemology, only the contents expressed in it. As a consequence, the conventional discourse misses the unique contribution of the act itself, an input not covered by the central functions of the psychoanalytic system.

Among psychoanalysts who have written about testimony in therapy, their focus has been on the role of the analyst as a witness and the power of testimony in the treatment of trauma. There are psychoanalysts who see its main importance at the beginning, at the stage of acquiring trust (Orange 1995), while others believe that its main value is towards the end of the treatment (Poland 2000), when the need arises to recognize the otherness of the patient.

This book argues that testimony in therapy is a distinct function, both on the part of the therapist and that of the patient, and its existence is important throughout the treatment and across the entire range of the psychic states in ways that go beyond its benefits in the treatment of trauma.

The Act of Testimony Is a Distinct Therapeutic Function

"Psychoanalysts are, above all, witnesses."[3]

Henry M. Seiden (1996)

The concept of testimony entered the clinical discourse in the nineties of the 20th century, a few years after the film "Shoah" by Claud Lanzman (1985) and in the wake of numerous publications of testimonies delivered by Holocaust survivors. As a result, the entry of the function into psychoanalysis was the outcome of a pre-occupation with trauma so that testimony and trauma were bound together.

This linkage involved the exercise of a double functions. On the one hand, trauma is very powerful (trauma always has the last word). This power has succeeded in spotlighting the therapeutic value of the function of testimony and removed it from its hideaway. On the other hand, this Gordian knot that has been formed, blurred other important features of testimony.

The objective of this book is to move the shadow of trauma from the phenomenon of testimony, especially in the therapeutic world, and to examine it as a whole phenomenon.

Testimony is an intersubjective act, since it is fundamentally addressed to another that will listen to it. In the absence of a listener, the testimony has no existence. This way, the experience of giving testimony in therapy involves both the patient and the therapist. The patient is a witness in that he gives his testimony about a real event that happened in his life and that he was there at the time. It could also be that his testimony relates to an internal emotional distress that is with him all the time.

This is first-hand testimony. The patient testifies about what happened to him or something he had witnessed. Often, in the course of giving testimony, things are revealed that he himself was unaware of.

And the therapist – he is a witness of a witness –listens to the first-hand testimony which took place in his presence and believes the story. This is second-hand testimony, but, at the same time, it's a first-hand testimony, given the physical and verbal scene which took place in the treatment room, where the patient gained recognition, and his testimony got validated. Both forms of testimony have a significant therapeutic value, and both serve the patient.

The distinctiveness of the function of testimony and witnessing in psychoanalysis is evident compared to other key analytic interventions. The obvious difference is the absence of any theoretical territory. Every other therapeutic function has a psychoanalytic theoretical backup. This is to say that every therapeutic function relies on one of the recognized psychoanalytic theories.

For example, 'interpretation' and 'transference' have their origins in 'classical' psychoanalysis. 'Projective identification', the 'depressive phase' or 'reparation' is to be found in Melanie Klein's theory. The concept of "good enough mother", the functions of containment and holding or the phenomenon of a "transitional object" have their origin in the Winnicottian school of thought, and both belong to the school of "object relations". 'Empathy', the 'self-object', 'mirroring' or 'ideal self' are embedded in Kohutian "self-psychology".

There are researchers such as Orange (1995) and Seiden (1996) who use the language of the "self-psychology" school and view the act of testimony as identical to, or as part of, other therapeutic functions such as 'empathy', 'mirroring' or 'self-object'. However, even though there are overlapping elements here, there is no identity.

The absence of theoretical support is, of course, a weakness, especially from the point of view of advancing the status of the function of testimony in psychoanalysis. But this is also an advantage because the lack of theoretical anchor enables the function of testimony to serve as an intermediary space, bridging two world views between which psychoanalysis wanders.[4]

The capacity of the function of witnessing to be an intermediary space or a 'third factor' is an actual advantage due to the contemporary tendency to moderate binary situations. Descriptions of this capacity are to be found in the writings of psychanalysts such as Stephen Mitchell and Lewis Aron (2013). Each, in their own way, mentioned many dichotomous situations in psychoanalysis – such as psychoanalysis and psychotherapy, object and subject or an inner and external reality – and recommended moderating them and engaging in more dialogues and mutual situations, maintaining, of course, the inherent asymmetry between therapist and patient in analytic therapy.[5]

Orange (1995) points to an additional unique aspect of testimony in psychoanalysis – which is the kind of interpretation it leads to. According to

Orange, the hermeneutic of testimony is "hermeneutic of trust."[6] But Clearly, this is not just simply a matter of trust. It is much more than that. This is the stage at which testimony comes in.

To be a witness is to listen and to believe through verbal and nonverbal communication.

List of References and Notes

1 Seiden, Henry M. (1996): "The Healing Presence. Part I: The Witness as Self-Object Function". *Psychoanalytic Review*, 83, p. 689.
2 The idea is borrowed from Laplanche (2001) where he discusses the development of thought and how that development differs in the field of psychoanalysis.
3 Seiden (1996), p. 690.
4 Wilson, Arnold (2003): "Ghosts of Paradigms Past: The Once and Future Evolution of Psychoanalytic Thought". *Journal of the American Psychoanalytic Association*, 51, pp. 825–855, 824.
5 Aron, Lewis (1996): *Meeting of Minds: Mutuality in Psychoanalysis*. The Analytic Press, Hillsdale, NJ.
6 Orange, Donna M. (1995): *Emotional Understanding: Studies in Psychoanalytic Epistemology*. The Guilford Press, New York and London.

Chapter 9

The History of Psychoanalysis's Attitude to the Testimonies of Patients

Zipi Rosenberg Schipper

In the chronicle of Psychoanalysis, there were some turns in the attitude towards patients' testimonies that moved from disbelief to fully trusting them. The turns were almost always in accordance with the worldviews that prevailed at that time.

The widespread view is that at the beginning of his analytic career, Freud fully trusted what his patients told him and took their words for granted and didn't distinguish between inner reality and external reality.

During his first treatments, he came to the conclusion that following the patients' associations up to the event, in which the symptoms of hysteria appeared for the first time, always led to a recollection of an incident of sexual abuse. Having accepted their testimonies as true, he formulated the "Theory of Seduction".

However, at a turning point in his thinking (1897), when the search for the etiology of the psychic disorder passed on, from an act that happened in reality to a search for the truth in fantasy, Freud began to listen to what his patients told him as wishful thinking and interpreted their words according to his preconceived assumptions.

Let us delve more deeply into this.

The 'Seduction theory' is the accepted term for a group of theories that guided Freud at the beginning of his way. His assumption was that the source of his female patients' neurotic hysteria was a trauma, generally sexual, they had experienced in their past. However, it transpired that not all the patients reported a sexual incident they had been subjected to. In such cases, Freud did not believe them and approached the data given him using an *a priori* theory with the objective of finding confirmation of his preconception.

For example, in the first phase of the 'Seduction theory', when the emphasis was on trauma and defense (1893–1894), Freud determined that the assumption must be an event that had occurred prior to the present event, which caused the hysteria, but he was not certain.

In regard to the footnote referring the letter Freud sent to Fleiss (17.1.1897), the editors point out that it:[1]

Hints of three important directions in which Freud's work was developed . . . the third is the collapse of Freud's view of the role of seduction in the etiology

DOI: 10.4324/9781003403920-11

of neuroses, which he was firmly convinced and continued to be convinced until in the course of his self-analysis, he suddenly realized the difference between phantasy and reality in what his patients told him. (p. 187)

A month later (8.2.1897), Freud wrote another letter in which he notes:

The theory has receded into the distance. I'm postponing all attempts to obtain understanding. Even the time relationships have begun to seem uncertain.

The response of the editors to this letter:

Freud was starting to feel that his old idea of the traumatic influence of seduction was no longer satisfactory.

On 2.5.1897, Freud wrote a note named "Architecture of Hysteria":

big advance . . . phantasies are psychical outworks constructed . . . they serve the purpose refining the memories . . . they combine things that have been experienced and things that have been heard about past events and things seen by the subject himself.

(pp. 197–198)

And in the footnote to this letter:

The big advance which Freud speaks, led to complete revision of his psychoanalytic hypothesis and turned it into psychology of instinct (p. 197).

Examining this turn is important to us because this was the moment that the real events became unimportant, which encouraged the attitude of doubt towards patients' testimonies.

In 1932, Freud wrote the following:

In the period in which the main interest was directed to discovering infantile sexual traumas, almost all my women patients told me that they had been seduced by their father. I was driven to recognize in the end, that these reports were untrue and so came to understand that hysterical symptoms are derived from fantasies and not from the occurrences.[2]

For many years this sentence reflected the essence of psychanalysis's attitude towards the testimonies of patients. The transition in Freud's thinking pointed to the notion that to believe what a patient was saying or to determine that the testimony expressed an external factual truth were two different processes.

Freud argued that the acceptance of the interpretation by his patient was perceived by him as confirming the correctness of the interpretation, and when subsequently the patient strongly rejected the interpretation, Freud regarded that also as confirmation of its correctness.[3]

The accepted approach to the Seduction theory was formulated by Freud's daughter, Anna Freud (1981), together with Ernest Jones (1953) and Ernst Krik. Freud held on to this theory for only a short time (estimated to have been between 2–4 years), and in 1897, he abandoned it in favor of the 'Oedipal' model, which places fantasy as the source of the neurosis. From that time on, Freud changed his approach and tended not to take his patients at their word.

Blas (2004) rejects the commonly accepted approach and claims that this view leans on a number of myths, though she emphasized that Freud contributed to this situation. In Blas's view, Freud did not change his method in any way; he checked the truth of the complaints and even testified that he tried to verify details given to him by relatives of patients. Secondly, Freud's disengagement from the seduction theory was not, in fact, clear-cut because more than having problems with the theory itself, he had difficulties with its foundation and the 'wild' way that characterized its conclusions.[4]

And indeed, in a letter Freud sent to Fliess (6.4.1897), p. 193, he wrote,

"The missing piece in the hysteria puzzle which I could not find has turned up in the form of a new source from which an element in unconscious production flows. I refer to the hysterical phantasies which, I now see, invariably go back to thigs heard in an early infancy and only subsequently understood" (p. 193).

In a letter two months before 8.2.1897, Freud admitted, "I am postponing all attempts to obtain understanding. Even the time relationships have begun to seem uncertain." (p. 192).

But the deed was done.

Freud's declared disavowal of the Seduction theory, whatever the reason may have been, had a far-reaching influence, during the 20th century, on the attitude of therapists to patients' testimonies. Generations of analysts who believed that they were following Freud's path treated patients with disbelief and skepticism.

For years, the approach of many analysts was that external facts, or the real events about which the patients were testifying, were so trivial that there was almost no meaning to the question of whether these events really happened or not. The testimonies of many patients were perceived as concealing the fantasies accompanying them. It was also in this spirit that Freud wrote his article "Screen Memories" (1919), in which he claimed that the memories raised in therapy were masking another truth.

The psychoanalyst who courageously went against the stream was Sándor Ferenczi (1932), Freud's contemporary, who was the first psychoanalyst to recognize the therapeutic virtues of the analyst's function as a witness.

Ferenczi was not supported by the psychoanalytic establishment of his time, supposedly because he deviated from Freud's way of thinking. However, ironically, today, he is regarded as one of the spiritual fathers of the 'Relational' theory, which conquered in the last two decades, and even before, a central place of the psychoanalytic world.

The process of change in the psychoanalytical attitude to testimony in therapy began with the development of the 'new approach' (1986) in the analytic field, which was mainly formulated by Jeffrey Masson (1994) and Alice Miller (1984.), who claimed that Freud's lack of belief to his patients was a "history of error."[5] In his book: *The Assault on Truth: Freud's Suppression of the Seduction Theory* (1984), Jeffrey Moussaieff Masson argues that Sigmund Freud made a mistake when he deliberately suppressed his early hypothesis, known as the seduction theory, that hysteria is caused by sexual abuse during infancy.

Reinforcement of this position took place already in the 1970s through Heinz Kohut, the founder of "self-psychology", and Carl Rogers, the founder of "Humanistic Psychology", both in the 1950s. They worked at the same time, chronologically, though detached from each other. Rogers had failed to be appreciated by the psychoanalytic establishment and remained under Kohut's shadow, who was extremely dominant in convincing the psychoanalytic community to adopt his ideas. Both advocated trusting a patient's testimony, but in completely different ways.

In his book, "*How does Analysis Cure?*" (1997), Kohut writes about the trust in what patients say:

> If there is one lesson that I have learned during my life as an analyst, it is the lesson that what my patients tell me is likely to be true – that many times when I *believed that I was right and my patients were wrong*, it turned out, though often only after a prolonged search, that *my* rightness was *superficial* whereas their rightness was *profound*[6]

> (Italics in the original.)

Carl Rogers (1978) believed in an even more extreme position as far as trust in what patients were telling him. He recognized the value of the therapist's position as a witness (without using the word 'witness'), and the basic principles underlying his doctrine match remarkably accurately with the principles of witnessing.

Rogers linked, as did Orange (1995) and Seiden (1996) many years later, careful listening to empathy. He believed that listening without making judgment means that you lay aside the views and values you hold for yourself in order to listen without prejudice (just like the "hermeneutic of trust", which is desired in listening to patients' testimonies).[7] In Rogers' view, the need to be known, by ourselves and others, even if only for a moment, is powerful.

He notes:

> It is astonishing how elements that seem insoluble become soluble, when someone listens, how confusions that seem irremediable turn into relatively clear flowing streams, when one is heard.[8]

Two decades later, new psychoanalytic schools have developed that were influenced by the ideas of 'post-modernism'. These new ideas led to an upheaval in the therapeutic paradigm and entirely altered the attitude towards patients' testimonies.

These approaches saw the great significance in the position that recognizes the value of the truth of the patient's testimony and honored the patient's external reality.

Blas (2004), who researched the changing attitude in psychoanalysis to testimonies of patients in the area of incest, attributes the altered view of testimony to the general changes in Western thought and, in particular, to the increasing power of the feminist movement.

Blass writes:

> The change that has occurred over the past two decades, is part of the general changes that have taken place in society, in which the feminist movements played a key role. In parallel there were internal developments in psychoanalysis that led to the strengthening of certain 'sub-approaches' such as "Self-psychology", the "Intersubjective" approach and the "Relational" approach, which offer a more central position to the actual external reality – be it the reality of the patient's life in the past and in the present, or be it the actual reality of the therapeutic situation itself, which is no longer conceived in terms of transference and counter-transference.[9]

This line of thinking has remained the guiding light to this day.

What Do We Mean When We Say "To Believe What Patients Tell Us?

The tendency to believe patients is today accepted by most analysts/therapists. But to what are we actually referring when we say that we believe what patients are saying to us?

- That the patient is being truthful?
- About what 'truth' are we talking about?

In order to answer these questions, we have to distinguish between two main streams of thought in psychoanalysis, among which there is disagreement in regard to these subjects.

The first stream places the mechanism of the 'unconscious' as being central to the theory and aspires to discover the unseen and hidden step behind the patient's associations. This applies to such cases as that of "Katrina" (1893), which is described as if it was a detective story, or the case of "Dora – An Analysis of a Case of Hysteria" (1905).

The analyst, in such cases, functions as a detective, who faces a multiplicity of confusing facts which were intended to conceal the truth, and his role is to unravel it. The 'truth', according to this approach, is, thus, perceived as something deep that cannot be discovered through the patient's first spoken experience.

The second stream emphasizes the experience of the patient, as it is expressed in the therapy. Such thinkers as Kohut (1977) and Winnicott (1970) adopt this approach. The truth is perceived as an experiential, emotional and subjective truth.

In these schools, there are profound interpretations that attempt to touch upon the unconscious. However, the therapist does not see himself as a detective looking for what lies behind what is being said. Rather, he sees his role as validating the emotional experiences of the patient. Such validation is dependent on trust. That is to say that it is accomplished only if the analyst believes the recounted experiences.

Trust, therefore, is not dependent on the truthfulness of the patient's claims but rather on the truth of the patient's subjective emotional experience. In order to strengthen this claim, we refer to Freud's article: "Mourning and Melancholia".

"Mourning and Melancholia"

Freud's article "Mourning and Melancholia" (1917) deals with the compatibility of the spoken personal experience with the actual reality. Following the stages of Freud's thinking in relation to this issue reveals the development of the perception of truth in psychoanalysis.

At the beginning of the article, Freud points out that as a person involves a greater degree of subjectivity in his recognition consciousness of the world, he distances himself from a more realistic perception of himself and of the other. However, in what follows, a gradual change is seen, and in the four stages of deliberations, he reaches a different surprising conclusion.

A Brief Summary of the Four Stages

- Both scientifically and therapeutically, it would be fruitless to contradict the patient who brings accusations against himself. He must surely be right in some way, but that, as we know, is secondary, as the effect of the inner travail consuming his ego, of which we know nothing but which we compare with the work of mourning.
- "In certain other self-accusations, he also seems to us justified, only that he has a keener eye for the truth than others who are not melancholic."
- "When in his exacerbation of self-criticism . . . whose sole aim has been to hide the weakness of his nature, for all we know it maybe that he has come very near to self-knowledge."[10]

In the final phase of his rethinking, Freud reached the conclusion that even worthy and good melancholics criticize themselves, and so the conclusion is that what the melancholic says is real. "This, from Freud's perspective", claims Govrin (2004), "was a revolutionary conclusion, because it suggested that it does not matter whether the subjective experience corresponds to an objective reality, since the "correspondence to reality, does not reflect its truth."[11]

The search for the kind of truth in psychoanalytic epistemology is awakened at times when there is a change of worldviews, which is a dominant factor in the construction of therapeutic theories.[12]

The philosophical problematics of the phenomenon of testimony, in general, also exists in testimony in therapy and, with it, the question of trust. One of the prominent researchers who considered the question of truth in therapy was Hanley (1990), and his writing reflects the nature of the thought process of other psychoanalytic researchers as well.

In the many debates that took place in relation to this issue, it seems clear that Hanley tends to accept the appropriateness of the belief that the testimony of patients should rely on the 'Correspondence Theory of the Truth'. However, the clinical work convinced him that the other theory, the 'Credibility Coherence Theory', is more applicable to therapy. Hanley points to an element of inner certainty that a man who testifies about himself has what very much resembles the arguments made by Felman and Laub (1992).

In his words:

> In the end, each person has only his own life to live, however shared with others. At the core of the being of each person there is a solitude in which he is related to himself. Truth resides in this solitude to the extent that one can remember one's own past as it actually was. The ground of genuine analytic work in the analyst, is his attitude of respect for this solitude.[13]

The therapeutic experience proves that the epistemological basis of the analyst who believes his patient's testimony can only be undermined if the analyst works in accordance with the "correspondence theory of truth" in its narrow sense (the reductionist approach). However, every perception of truth in which the context of testimony is included (as in the non-reductionist approach) and in which the subject's experiences, emotions and motives are considered suits clinical work. Therapists who lack confidence in the truth of what their patient is saying are mistaken in their approach.[14]

It has to be pointed out that the question of whether a patient's experience should be taken into account or only the truthfulness of his testimony is an ancient question that has been discussed by philosophers for hundreds of years, as have psychoanalysts since the inception of the discipline. In the field of psychology, the debate mainly revolves around the issue of the external reality's place in the therapeutic theory.[15]

Another interesting question, which I will not deal with here in any depth, is "What is the perception of truth accepted by therapists, and what are the considerations on which this perception is based?"

The apparent answer is that in his treatment room, every analyst mostly works on the basis of the training he received, his intuition, in line with the 'spirit of the times', but, especially according to the experience of the analyst that his actions are 'working'.

Such an approach expresses the "pragmatic" stream, according to which thoughts, expressed ideas or world views are tools that enable one to achieve the objectives of one's life. The pragmatic stream believes that to believe works!

This pragmatic perception of truth was formulated by William James (1907), who spoke in a profound way of the will to believe as being man's primary wish. "This notion role serves not only the principle of meaning, but also the principle of truth".[16]

In James's terms, the difference between believing and being skeptical is that the first leads to the success of the action, whilst the second is liable to bring about its failure. In his words:

> True faith about the way out of the forest, will indeed lead the way to the exit, whereas a false belief will cause the person to continue to wander in the forest.[17]

Three Positions and a Call for Change

In light of this discussion, there appear to be three positions along the axis of time in the attitude of psychoanalysis towards testimonies of patients, which shift from disbelief to total trust and to an additional position that is more complex.

The first position, influenced by Freud and his successors, claims that conscious testimony blurs unconscious contents and that the analyst's main role is to track such contents.

The second position, formulated by the 'Object Relations' and 'self-psychology' theories of Winnicott and Kohut, had the attitude towards patients' testimonies reversed, and therapists tended to believe everything their patients told them.

The third position is more complex. The first researchers to represent it were Alice Miller (1991) and Judi Herman (1992). In parallel to them, it was expressed by Shoshana Felman and Dori Laub. Subsequently, researchers from the "Intersubjective" and "Relational" schools of thought supported this view. The prominent among them were Henry Seiden (1996), Warren Poland (2000), Donna Orange (1996), Chana Ulman (2006) and Lewis Aron (2013). This position views the patient's testimony in therapy as an important function by virtue of the fact that the analyst is a witness, listening to the patient's experiences and, in doing so, validates the patient's perception of his traumatic past.

I call here for a reformulation of the third position, a formulation that will recognize the act of testimony and witnessing as an essential tool for a psychic change in every form of therapy, regardless of the contents raised in it, one which is not limited to patients who have endured a traumatic experience.

List of References and Notes

1 Freud, Sigmund (1887–1902): *The Origins of Psycho-Analysis: Letters to Wilhelm Fliess, Drafts and Notes* (ed. Marie Bonaparte, Anna Preud and Ernst Kris). Basic Books, Inc. Publishing, New York, 3, pp. 187–198 (1954).

2 Freud, Sigmund (1932), "New Introductory Lectures on Psychoanalysis". *S.E.*, 22, p. 120.

3 Blas, Rachel (2004): "The History of Psychoanalysis's Attitude to Incest". In: *The Secret and Its Breaking: Issues in Incest* (ed. C. Seligman and Solomon). Hakibbuts Hameuchad Publishing, Bnei Brak, Israel, pp. 433–456, 445 (Hebrew).

4 Ibid., p. 450.

5 Masson, Jeffrey Moussaieff (1984): *The Assault on Truth: Freud's Suppression of the Seduction Theory*. Farrar, Straus and Giroux, New York, NY. ISBN 978-0345452795.

6 Kohut, Heinz (1997): *How Does Analysis Cure?* University of Chicago Press, Chicago, IL, pp. 93–94.

7 Orange, M. Donna (2011): *The Suffering Stranger: Hermeneutics For Everyday Clinical Practice*. Routledge/Taylor & Francis, New York.

8 Rogers, Carl (1995): *A Way of Being*. Houghton Mifflin Harcourt, Boston, p. 30.

9 Blass Rachel (2004), pp. 433–456, 451 (Hebrew).

10 Freud, Sigmund (1917): "Mourning and Melancholia". Sigmund Freud, Collected Papers, Vol. IV, pp. 152–170.

11 Govrin, Aner (2004): *Between Abstinence and Seduction*. Kinneret-Zmora-Bitan-Dvir – Publishing House Ltd, Or-Yehuda, Israel, p. 52. (Hebrew).

12 Hanley, Carl (1990): "The Concept of Truth in Psychoanalysis". *International Journal of Psycho-Analysis*, 71, pp. 375–383.

13 Ibid., pp. 381–382.

14 There are many examples of this in the history of psychoanalysis, like *"Dora"* – *Fragment of an Analysis of a Case of Hysteria* (1905 [1901]), of Sigmund Freud (The Standard Edition of the Complete Psychological Works of Sigmund Freud, Volume VII (1901–1905): In *Three Essays on Sexuality and Other Works*, pp. 1–122. but dealing additional theories of such instances would be too great a deviation from the subject.

15 Blass, Rachel (2004), p. 252.

16 William, James (1995): *Pragmatism*. Dover Publications Inc, New York, USA (1997), p. 18.

17 Ibid., p. 15.

Chapter 10

Recognizing the Power of the Function of Testimony in Therapy

Zipi Rosenberg Schipper

Introduction

An entire century of psychoanalytic thought passed by, before psychoanalysis came to recognize the therapeutic power of testimony.

Psychoanalysis had gone through two world wars. The First World War (1914–1917) was horrendous and long, but it didn't suppress the development of ideas in the various fields of knowledge. On the contrary, during and especially after the war had ended, there was a fertile philosophical and psychological creativity that altered human consciousness until today.

Freud continued his intensive development of the psychoanalytic model in parallel to – and sometimes in conjunction with – recognized philosophers like Husserl, Heidegger, Wittgenstein and others, who shaped Western thought throughout the 20th century and continue to do so. This was not the case in the aftermath of World War II. Under the shadow of that war and the horror of the Shoah, a mood of silence prevailed.

After World War II, the world of philosophy was muted. This 'Philosophy's silence' lasted for years until it found a lexicon of its own. The philosophy's late response was expressed in the terms formulated by the 'post-modernist' movement and the 'Deconstruction', which broke accepted conventions and the ideas that until then had been unacceptable, became appropriate and vice versa.

Ben Naftali (1993), who searched the philosophic changes after World War II, writes:

> The presentation of deconstruction as the philosophy of the Shoah is likely to be viewed as strange . . . However, anyone looking closely at Deconstruction, in the world of values, which it chose to shatter or undermine, . . . will discover that the horrendous meeting between man and Auschwitz, became the axis of philosophy's revisionism, or better still, the cultural-critical revision of man's attachment to himself, to his fellow man and to his world.[1]

It also happened in psychoanalysis.

According to Lewis Aron (2015), psychanalysis could be regarded as having been a holocaust survivor itself and has not discussed the Shoah sufficiently as a trauma that needs to be addressed. According to Aron, psychoanalysis acted via

DOI: 10.4324/9781003403920-12

manic defenses, whose origins were to be found in the death anxiety which accompanied the outcomes of the war. Even "Ego Psychology", which was the dominant psychoanalytic theory in the years after the war, was an omnipotent defense mechanism.[2]

The idea noted here is that the recognition of the importance of the function of testimony in therapy and the interest it has lately aroused in the psychoanalytic narrative, mainly in the context of trauma, is a part, or a direct outcome, of the 'philosophy's silence' and the psychoanalytic state of shock.

In a way that is similar to the body image phenomenon, that alters a great deal after the physical changes have already taken place, so a change in the 'knowledge image' of a concept gains recognition only after a significant lapse of time when the alteration has already occurred.

As said, change in the image of knowledge mainly develops in the social arena, but the change only becomes recognized in the context of a development of a new and relevant philosophic idea. Meaning that there is a direct connection between a general undermining of conventions in the world of philosophy and the ability to perceive the function of testimony from a different perspective.

In addition, there is a direct link between the establishment of institutions and organizations across the globe, in these years, devoted to hearing the testimonies of Shoah survivors and the entry of the concept of testimony into the psychoanalytic narrative, which in many ways, the conceptual changes made room for it.

The concept of testimony in therapy was, as said, bound up in an immediate way with the phenomenon of trauma; therefore, the first stage in the recognition of the importance of testimony was the understanding of its power in the treatment of trauma (Boulanger 2005). Unfortunately, psychoanalytic testimonial discourse still continues to be conducted through this prism.

The objective of this book is to broaden the recognition of the scope of that ability of the function of testimony, to recognize its importance in psychic change and its therapeutic power in every psychological and psychoanalytic treatment, regardless of its c specific contents.

Among other changes following the shift in world views that influenced the formation of new psychoanalytic schools of thought, two significant turns in therapeutic practice occurred:

- A change in the perception of the unconscious.
- A change in the perception of the analyst's therapist's role.

The Change in the Perception of the Unconscious

The mechanism of the 'unconscious', which is the term most identified with psychoanalysis and which changed the perception of human consciousness, expresses, in essence, a principled skepticism in the visible consciousness.

While working, Freud understood that many psychic phenomena in an individual or in society and even in culture and art almost never derive from cognitive or perceptual errors. Rather, they stem from the defense mechanism tasked with the non-recognition of external and internal reality as it is.

According to Freud's 'Drive' theory, the 'Unconscious' is revealed indirectly. In Freud's time, and for a number of generations after him, analysts saw in the 'unconscious' the 'otherness' that exists in every individual and which is not easy to reach. This perception has undergone a number of changes.

The attitude of the contemporary psychoanalytic schools to 'the Unconscious' has changed. Although their theories do not cancel the concept of 'the unconscious', they do differ in their attitude towards it.

Govrin (2004), in his book "*Between Abstinence and Seduction*", noted that in the Intersubjective and the Relational approaches, "The position of the 'Unconscious', is undermined and emptied of its contents."[3] In his article "The Dilemma of Contemporary Psychoanalysis: Toward a 'Knowing' Post-Postmodernism" (2006), Govrin claims that these alterations were influenced by Post-modern thought, arguing that "Postmodern psychoanalysis changed the ideal of the analyst who 'knows', with an analyst who acknowledges uncertainty and embraces the impossibility of recognizing only *one* truth".[4]

Orange (1995), on the other hand, claims that the ideological philosophers such as Buber, Wittgenstein, Gadamer or Levinas were the ones who influenced the epistemology of the 'Intersubjective' and 'Relational' schools. And similarly to Govrin, Orange argues that, analysts who were the 'knowers' are now the analysts who are allowed 'not to know'.

Orange notes about the role of the therapist after the change:

> Perhaps the most striking shift comes in the rejection of "clear" and distinct ideas in favor of the chaos, complexity, more-or-less quality, and general fallibilism of systems thinking. . . . we can rely on our emotional contexts enough to tolerate the endlessly open question. Such a capacity in the clinician must surely reassure the patient, more than any clear and distinct answers.[5]

Heinz Kohut (1959)[6] was the first one to openly express this change. In his writings, he attributes a lesser importance to the concept of the unconscious and considers it to be due to changes in worldviews. What was concealed and hidden in Freud's time, especially in sexual matters, claims Kohut, is accepted in his own time in greater openness.

According to Kohut, invasive interpretation is inappropriate in therapy and proposes active listening. In his view, "only the analyst's willingness to be an attentive silent listener will be tolerable to the patient"[7] Similarly, in Donna Orange's Intersubjective model, which she terms "Perspectival Realism", the analyst and the analysand share their knowledge and opinions with each other.

She notes:

> Perspectival realism recognizes that the only truth or reality, to which psychoanalysis provides access, is the subjective organization of experience understood in an intersubjective context . . . Kohut's self-psychology views subjectivity as the entire domain of psychoanalysis . . . While this view does exclude common-sense realism, correspondence theories of truth, and scientific empiricism, it does not exclude the possibility of dialogues, communication, or perspectival realism . . . self-correcting process only partly accessible via personal subjectivity but increasingly understandable in communitarian dialogue.[8]

A unique view is expressed by Julia Kristeva in her book: "*Tales of Love*" (2009). In Kristeva's view, the unconscious is not an inaccessible entity that an individual finds hard to enter. Rather, it is an entity that is in a constant dialogue with the conscious part of that person's psyche, and it is this dialogue that gives meaning to what is being said.[9]

The Change in the Role of the Analyst/Therapist

As part of the crystallization of the new schools of thought, there has been a dramatic change in the nature of the relations between the analyst/therapist and the analysand/patient. The previously accepted view was to see the relations between the two as relations between object and subject. Today, they are viewed as relations between subjects.

The therapeutic practice has transitioned from a monadic model, which is to say, a framework of 'one person psychology' – expressing a perception that sees the individual as a closed system propelled by inner drives, which is mainly the traditional classical psychoanalysis – into a 'two persons psychology' – a therapeutic approach that focuses on characterizing the interaction between the therapist and the patient. As Stephen Mitchell (2016) writes: "This interaction is the space within which most of the contemporary analytic theorization operates."[10]

In her article "From Cartesian minds to experiential worlds in psychoanalysis",[11] Orange offers a philosophical explanation for these developments. In Orange's view, there are eight contradictions between Cartesian lines of thought, which greatly influenced Freud's thinking, and the assumptions rooted in the alternative concept of the experimental world that is characterized by the post-positivist epistemology.

Orange writes:

> Decart's "*Mediations*", developed over the modern era, into the mental mechanism in the work of Freud. Although Freud's systematic study of unconscious processes undermined an important component of the Cartesian, namely its devotion to clear and distinct ideas . . . the psychoanalytic mind has been and

continues to be the Cartesian mind. For most of us, the entire complex of pre-suppositions that I'm calling Cartesian mind is largely unconscious, embedded in the underlying grammar of our Western work and continues to characterize our psychoanalytic and philosophical thinking.[12]

Eight contrasts are drawn between the characteristics of the Cartesian mind and the assumption embedded in the alternative conception of an experimental world. The Cartesian mind is isolated and self-sufficient, subject opposed to object, inner, devoted to clear-and-distinct ideas, reliant on true-false logic, atemporal, representational and substantial. Experimental world is relational social, dialogic, and contextual, perspectival, inhabited and inhabiting, complex and fallibilistic, more or less aware, temporal and emergent, understanding oriented and organizing process.[13]

In her description of the various changes, Orange notes that she provides therapists whose approach has already changed intuitively but who are also interested in the philosophical anchor to their practice.

Orange writes:

The Cartesian mind is isolated and self-enclosure, there is a split between subject and object, a dichotomy between inner reality to external reality, devoted to clear-and-distinct ideas, reliant on true-false logic, atemporal, representational, and substantial.

Experimental world is relational, social, dialogic, and contextual, perspectival, inhabited and inhabiting, complex and fallibilistic, more or less aware, temporal and emergent, understanding oriented and organizing process.[14]

All those turns affected psychoanalytic thinking and provided a theoretical basis for the shift of the relationships in the treatment situation and in changing the perception of the therapist's role.

Among other changes, Orange describes variations that, to a great extent, are responsible for the upgrading of the status of the function of testimony in therapy. For example, the split between object and subject, the dichotomy between inner and external reality, as well as the need for presumptions have been changed into a dialogic, perspectival and contextual world that encourages processes and in which mistakes are permissible.

The Significant Reasons for *Not* Recognizing Testimony as a Therapeutic Function

In contrast to the unsurprising non-recognition of the significance of the act of testimony in the field of philosophy, when it comes to the therapeutic field, such non-recognition is a highly startling fact. Looking back, there are profound reasons as to why a clear therapeutic function, such as testimony, has not been acknowledged in psychoanalysis.

One of the main reasons was that Freud – the father of psychoanalysis – was unwilling to adopt a function that was not at one with the scientific world. Freud never gave up his desire to display the psychoanalytic theory as having scientific qualities, and the act of testimony lacks scientific qualities.

An additional reason is linked to Freud's refusal to adopt a concept that originated in a religious tradition, and the sources of testimony are, as said, based on the holy scriptures. Freud understood that the connotations rooted in the concept of testimony (that God witnesses man and that man witnesses God, or that testimony is linked to prophecy and possesses some kind of mysticism and a sort of divinity) would allow entry into the treatment room something which did not fit in with the nature of psychoanalysis as Freud wished it to.

In his 35th lecture (1933) on "The Question of a world view" (*weltanschauung*), Freud argued that psychanalysis would not be able to form a worldview of its own. In order to establish its theory, Freud had to lean on a recognized worldview external to his own doctrine. He chose the scientific way.

> A depth psychology or psychology of the unconscious – it is quite unfit to construct a *Weltanschauung* of its own: It must accept the scientific one . . . religion alone is to be taken seriously as an enemy.[15]

Anything that was not in keeping with the scientific view was not worthy of consideration. (This despite the fact that he established a theory in which there are many elements of religious dogma.) Freud was contemptuous of philosophical thought (despite the fact that in constructing his theory, he was nourished a great deal by philosophical thinking).

Orange (2011) reinforcers this claim and argues that psychoanalysis was born and developed by a rejection of and opposition to the world of religion. Also Aron (2011) argues that "Freud regarded religion as something infantile and unwanted; that it encourages worthless illusions and that it is filled with irrational questions."[16]

The epistemological implication of this view is to cast doubt on anything that is not uttered by the individual himself or proven by science. This is how the attitude to the standing of the therapist – as a witness to the testimonies of patients, as being complex and uncertain – was determined.

This explains psychoanalysis's wavering relations over many years to the function of testimony in therapy.

List of References and Notes

1 Ben Naftali, B. Michal (1993): "The Israeli Philosophers and the Shoah". *Theory and Critisism*. The Van Leer Institute, Israel, 4, pp. 57–78, p. 70 (Hebrew).
2 In a lecture: "Psychanalysis as a Holocaust Surviver" by Lewis Aron in "Maagalim" (Circles) Conference (2013), Tel-Aviv, which appears also in the book by Aron, Lewis and Starr, Karen E. (2012): A Psychotherapy for the People: Towards a Progressive Psychoanalysis (Hapter Book Series), Chapter 7. Routledge, New York, NY.

3 'Govrin, Aner (2004): *Between Abstinence and Seduction.* Kinneret, Zmora-Bitan, Dvir – Publishing House Ltd., Or-Yehuda, Israel, p. 154. Hebrew.

4 Govrin, Aner (2006): "The Dilemma of Contemporary Psychoanalysis: Toward a 'Knowing' Post-Postmodernism". *Journal of the American Psychoanalytic Association,* 54 (2), p. 507.

5 Orange, M. Donna (2001): "From Cartesian Minds to Experimental Worlds in Psychoanalysis". *Psychoanalytic Psychology,* 18 (2), pp. 287–302, 297, 298–299.

6 Kohut, Heinz (1959): "Introspection, Empathy, and Psychoanalysis: An Examination of the Relationship between Mode of Observation and Theory". *Journal of the American Psychoanalytic Association,* 7, pp. 459–483.

7 Kohut, Heinz (1984): *How Does Analysis Cure?* University of Chicago Press, Chicago, IL, p. 177.

8 Orange, Donna M. (2011): *The Suffering Stranger: Hermeneutics for Everyday Clinical Practice.* Routledge/Taylor & Francis, New York, p. 62.

9 Kristeva, Julia (1987): Tales of Love. Columbia University Press, New York, NY (1987).

10 Mitchell, A. Stephen (1988): *Relational Concepts in Psychoanalysis.* Harvard University Press, Cambridge, MA.

11 Orange (2001), pp. 297, 298–299.

12 Ibid., p. 288.

13 Ibid., p. 287.

14 Ibid.

15 Freud, Sigmund (1933): "Lecture XXXV the Question of a Weltanschauung". *S.E.,* 22, pp. 158–160. Published by the Hogarth Press Limited by Arrangement with George Allen and Unwin Ltd, London, England.

16 Aron, Lewis (2011): "A Commentary to Sue Grand's Paper: God at an Impasse". Unpublished manuscript, p. 37.

Chapter 11

A Review of the Writings of Psychoanalytic Researchers on the Function of Testimony in Therapy

Zipi Rosenberg Schipper

Introduction

The following review includes researchers and analysts who recognized testimony, in and of itself, as being worthy of appreciation and acknowledgment and who expanded their investigation of the subject beyond the tie between testimony and trauma, thereby contributing to the deciphering of the phenomenon of spoken testimony. Thus, important researchers such as Lifton (2011), Boulanger (2005), Ullman (2006), Grant (2011), and others that saw the need for testimony only when the treatment involves trauma are not included.

Having said that, it should be noted that a significant part of the review is in the spirit of the psychoanalytic discourse on testimony, which revolves around the link between trauma and testimony and focuses, for the most part, on the role of the analyst as a witness.

With the exception of Ferenczi, in the first third of the 20th century, and Rogers, in the second third, who wrote on the therapeutic advantages of the therapist functioning as a witness (without really using the word testimony or witnessing), the psychoanalysts who wrote about testimony in therapy, did it only in the last decade of the 20th century. This chapter reviews their writings in chronological order.

Sándor Ferenczi

The first psychoanalyst to recognize the value of the function of testimony in the process of therapy was Sándor Ferenczi. In his "Clinical Diary" (1932), he describes the position of the analyst as a witness and the contribution of this position in building mutual trust, and in the validation of an event, by acknowledging the feelings of the patient.

He writes:

> It appears that patients cannot believe that an event really took place, or cannot fully believe it, if the analyst, as the sole witness of the events, persists in his cool, unemotional, and, as patients are fond of stating, purely intellectual attitude, while the events are of a kind that must evoke, in anyone present, emotions

DOI: 10.4324/9781003403920-13

of revulsion, anxiety, terror, vengeance, grief and the urge to render immediate help: to remove or destroy the cause or the person responsible . . . and since it is usually a child, an injured child . . . feelings of wanting to comfort him with love. . . .

One therefor has a choice: to take really seriously the *role* one assumes, of the benevolent and helpful observer, that is, actually to transport oneself with the patient into the period of the past (a practice Freud reproached me for, as being not permissible), with the result that we ourselves and the patient believe in its **reality**,[1] that is, a present reality, which has not been momentarily transported into the past . . . But if we adopt this view, and contrive right from the beginning to present the events to the patient as memory images, that are unreal in the present, he may well follow our line of thought, but will remain on an intellectual level, without ever attaining the feeling of conviction . . . The patient prefers to doubt his own judgment, rather than believe in our coldness, our lack of intelligence, or, in simpler terms, our stupidity and nastiness.[2]

In another place (8.8.1932), in the context of the therapist as a witness, Ferenczi writes about the need of the patient to get recognition from the analyst.

He writes:

What she now expects from me is:

(1) Belief in the reality of the incident.
(2) Reassurance that I consider her innocent.
(3) Innocent, even if it would appear that she derived great satisfaction from the attack and repaid her father with admiration.
(4) The certainty that I will not let myself be carried away by similar passionate behavior.[3]

With this, Ferenczi succeeded in encompassing the significant outlines of testimony in therapy:

• Complete trust in what the patient told him.
• Attributing importance to the actual situation, the external reality of the story and of the testimony, as well as of the therapeutic situation.
• Being non-judgmental.
• Abstaining from transference interpretation.
• Removing the fear of the results of giving testimony.
• The treatment room as a 'safe place'.

Ferenczi's important statements in the context of testimony in therapy are a comprehensive description of the function. The recognition of the importance of the position of the analyst as a witness, which Ferenczi pointed to in the 1930s, came to be accepted only sixty years later!

Alice Miller

And indeed, only in the last decade of the 20th century, psychoanalysts began to write about the power of testimony in alleviating distress. The first of them who recognized witnessing as a distinct therapeutic function was Alice Miller (1991). A few years after the screening of the movie "Shoah", when there was a preoccupation with the traumas of the war, Miller investigated the vital role of a witness in human life and especially children's lives.

In her book "*The Untouched Key*" (1991), which deals with both children and adults, Miller (similarly to Ferenczi) argues that a child who has been abused, in the absence of any witness, does not have the ability to be in touch with his emotional world, and even to acknowledge that he had been abused.

Miller writes about the role of testimony in people's lives in general and in psychoanalytic therapy in particular. She even links the two. She makes the connection between going to therapy and having witnesses in a person's life and argued that a person who has endured prolonged suffering in his life, when there were no witnesses to acknowledge his distress, loses, even in adulthood, the capacity to enjoy relationships with other people or to benefit from therapy.[4]

Miller emphasizes that "The presence of a witness in the life of a person who endures abuse, prevents the harsh consequences of trauma and ensures a better rehabilitation."[5]

Judith Lewis Herman

At the same time, chronologically speaking, Herman worked with post-traumatic adults and made a decisive contribution to the recognition of the therapeutic power of the act of testimony.

In her book, "*Trauma and Recovery*" (1992),[6] Herman draws desired technical lines for the therapist as a witness. She attributes significant value to the concerned listening of the addressee – the witnessing therapist – by providing the addressor – the patient – with a stage and avoids interventions and diagnoses during the testimony. In the main, Herman seeks to be assisted by patience and avoid premature closure.

In her words:

> Both patient and therapist must develop tolerance for some degree of uncertainty, even regarding the basic facts of the story. The story may change as missing pieces are recovered. . . . In order to resolve her own doubts or conflicting feelings, the parent may sometimes try to reach premature closure . . . Therapists, too, sometimes fall prey to the desire for certainty . . . The therapist has to remember that she is not a fact finder and that the reconstruction of the trauma story, is not a criminal investigation. Her role is to be an open-minded compassionate witness, not a detective.
>
> Because the truth is so difficult to face, survivors often vacillate in reconstructing their stories. Denial of reality makes them feel crazy, but acceptance of

the full reality seems beyond what any human being can bear . . . Psychotherapy, however, does not get rid of the trauma. The goal of recounting the trauma story is integration, not exorcism. In the process of reconstruction, the story does undergo a transformation, but only in the sense of becoming more present and more real . . . In telling the truth, the trauma story becomes a testimony.[7]

Careful listening, in Herman's view, facilitates the construction of the missing narrative that is essential to the integrity of the 'self'. The witness's listening turns the missing part into something meaningful.

Herman attributes differing dimensions to the act of testimony, one of which is the ceremonial aspect. According to Herman, people turn to therapy in an attempt to rid themselves of traumatic memories. However, this image of catharsis or exorcism is also an implicit fantasy in many traumatized patients who seek treatment.

Judith Herman quotes Inger Agger and Soren Jensen, who refers to the universality of testimony as a ritual of healing and points to both sides of personal testimony and their union.[8]

Testimony has both a private dimension which is confessional and spiritual, and a public aspect, which is political and judicial. The use of the word 'testimony', links both meanings, giving a new and larger dimension to the patient's individual experience.[9]

Later on, Judith Herman quotes Richard Molica,[10] he claimed that telling the trauma story makes it a new story that is no longer about shame and humiliation but rather about dignity and virtue. He notes that through their storytelling, refugee patients "regain the world they have lost."[11]

Miller and Herman are the most quoted researchers in the psychoanalytic testimonial discourse, and most researchers use their writings as a starting point in the way they think about testimony.

Shoshana Felman and Dori Laub

In an almost parallel time zone, Shoshana Felman and Dori Laub describe in their book "*Testimony: The Crisis of Witnessing in Literature, Psychoanalysis and History*"[12] (1992) the crisis that Holocaust survivors endured and continue to endure. They defined "our era is the era of testimony"[13] – a prophecy that has been realized in every area of knowledge and society. Their reference to the act of testimony is comprehensive and includes many philosophical and literal aspects, and is not specific to the therapeutic field.

Felman and Laub have contributed greatly to the discourse of testimony in the world. Their writing appears throughout this book, and there is no need to add any further comment here.

Donna Orange

Donna Orange, philosopher and Intersubjective psychoanalyst, deals a lot in the nature of the relationships between patient – analyst/therapist in the treatment room. In her book "*Emotional Understanding*" (1995), Orange attempts to find a new philosophical framework for psychoanalysis and devotes an entire chapter to spelling out the importance of the function of testimony and witnessing in psycho-analytic treatment. The chapter is titled "Better Late than Never: The Emotionally Available Witness".[14]

The sources of Orange inspiration are rooted in the 'self-psychology' school and supported by various dialectic philosophers such as Ricker (1970), Gadamer (2004), Buber (1970), Levinas (1971) and others.

In Orange's view, the act of witnessing derives from the functions of mirror-ing and 'self-object'. She notes that 'self-psychology' considered 'mirroring' as an essential requirement that is vital to the cohesiveness of the self and to the sense of positive self-worth.

In her words:

> I wish to draw attention to a selfobject experience – closely related to mirroring – particularly involved in psychoanalytic healing . . . – selfobject experience of wit-ness . . . A special form of participation in the intersubjective field, makes the other's experience real and valid.[15] This witnessing is indeed a subset of mirroring if mirror-ing means appreciative response to what is valuable in the child.[16]

Orange believes that the therapist, as a witness, has the power and the ability to call things by their name, which gives them existence.

> The analyst or therapist who wants to understand what happened to the child whose adult self, comes for treatment – becomes the witness who makes it pos-sible for the adult to experience . . . his or her history and thus to begin to heal. What we often call denial, disavowal or unconsciousness may often be experi-ence as never truly experienced.[17] . . .
>
> Witnessing means the presence of a responsive person who makes it possible for a child, or a patient who was the child, to recognize the horror of whatever happened to him, or her, and to feel the pain.[18]

That is – in the presence of validating witness, the child can experience the abuse as mistreatment and, thereby, find ways to express it.

Orange points out that 'our' inclination as analysts is to put the patient's trauma 'on hold'. However, she emphasizes that the testimony, having been delivered, requires that we do not put it aside. We have to be prepared to bear witness to the traumas of our patients. The act of testimony is not characterized by neutrality; it's a special form of cooperation in the intersubjective field, which includes a mixture of listening and attentiveness and excludes judgment. In this way, Orange argues that witnessing "undoes dissociation and allows a person to establish the continuity of a self-possessed life. It undoes shame and restores the positive valuation of the self." To reinforce her view, Orange quotes Winnicott from *Playing and Reality* (1971), that it needs the responsive emotionality of the intersubjective field or potential space, to allow it to become real and meaningful experience.[19]

The patient, in other words, can experience raw pain but needs the responsive other to construe it, to understand its enormity and meaning. In Orange's view, the analyst and patient make sense of it together.

Another significant aspect that Orange emphasizes in the function of testimony is the kind of interpretation that is rooted in the act of witnessing. According to Orange, all interpretations in psychoanalysis have to be like the interpretation of testimony – which is based on 'hermeneutic of trust' (hermeneutics is the study of interpretation) (Orange 2011). The analyst as a witness does not proceed in the accepted way, which Ricoeur somewhat vaguely termed as a 'hermeneutic of suspicion'. Nor does the analyst relate to the therapeutic text laid out in the traditional way as 'the text that is in another place'. Rather, he/she believes that this is the way things are and that there is no need to search for a hidden meaning. The 'interpretation of suspicion', according to Orange, leaves the patient alone in the room. Orange emphasizes that the witness (the analyst) has to have full trust in the testifier so that he doesn't remain alone:

The hermeneutics of trust assumes that we (patient and therapist, or any interlocutors in conversation) belong to a common human world, to traditions (both similar and different) and history (including traumatic history), and intend to seek understanding within it. . . . With dialogue or conversation. When we find ourselves in a misunderstanding, we attempt to give each other the benefit of the doubt.[20]

And later on:

The hermeneutics of trust invites less defensiveness, as it understands resistance and defense, as absolutely needed modes of coping with unbearable traumatic terrors and lonely anxieties. Gradually such a hermeneutics makes a relational home (Stolorow, 2007) for previously unwitnessed traumatic experience.[21]

In the book "*The Suffering Stranger*" (2011), Orange writes:

I believe, taking the risk of trusting the patient to be telling his or her truth as best possible (Orange, 2011), allows the clinician to become the needed "Moral witness" (Margalit, 2002).[22]

Moreover, Orange claims that an element of interpretation is an inherent part of listening itself, and that is, without doubt, a psychoanalytic act, she notes:

> Close listening is in itself an important form of interpretation . . . and fully deserves to be considered psychoanalytic[23]

Henry Seiden

Henry Seiden is the best advocate of the act of testimony. In his view, "Parents, and friends and lovers, and psychoanalysts are self-objects. They are also witnesses. They see, record, name, validate, care about and take responsibility for what they witness".[24]

In his article "The Healing Presence: The Witness as Self-Object Function" (1996), Seiden investigates the roles of the act of witnessing in people's lives in general and in therapy in particular. Seiden and Orange speak similar language, the 'intersubjective' language, which, from many points of view, derives from the language of 'self-psychology' school, which links the function of testimony in therapy to the functions of self-object,[25] empathy and mirroring.

Furthermore, Seiden argues that from the outset, the meaning of empathy was not clear-cut, and with the passage of time, its definition became increasingly vague.

He notes:

> The function of testimony is what Kohut was referring to as the therapeutic function of 'empathy'. Perhaps his dilemma would have been solved by limiting the meaning of the term, 'empathy', to the process of apprehending the experience of another person and understanding that the stance of the analyst as witness is the curative factor.[26]

In his investigation, Seiden goes beyond the tie of testimony and trauma and attempts to obtain a more complete picture of the act of witnessing and argues (as Orange does) that every person needs the presence of another individual to witness him in order to understand what is happening to him.

In his words:

> It seems safe to say that coherent experience – to perceive what is and to think straight about it – requires . . . the confirming presence of other people. To believe in and trust what one sees, requires a sense that another person in the same place and at the same time, would see the same thing, the same way. We need the sense that our experience is shared in order to feel that our reasoning is firm, that what we know to be true is true, that what we feel is valid. . . . it is the confirming presence of others which allows us to go on believing that we are who we think we are. All of which is to say that a coherent self requires, explicitly or implicitly, its witnesses.[27]

Seiden emphasizes that "The presence of a witness is a necessary condition of growth and the absence is a painfully lonely state which threatens the cohesion of self."[28]

After illustrating his claim via two case studies, in which he shows the importance of the therapist being a witness, Seiden goes one step further and asks therapists to be the witness that the patient has not had in his life: "I hope that these two cases can be seen as representative of many in showing that the analyst can provide for each patient the specific kind of witness that the patient was deprived of earlier in life."[29]

Thereafter, Seiden searches the sources of testimony and the unique connotations with which it has been stamped. In his view, the concept of testimony is taken from two fields – the religious tradition and the judicial world – and it reached psychoanalysis already charged with emotional and cognitive meanings from those domains, and these dictate its role in psychoanalytic treatment.

More specifically, the Jewish tradition expresses the idea of the constant, protective and mutual experience, in which God is witness to man and man is witness to God: "Even when I walk in the valley of darkness, I will fear no evil for You are with me; Your rod and Your staff –they comfort me" (Psalms 23).

Seiden even attributes it to civil rights:

> The Bible itself consists of "testaments" – of human beings affirming and testifying to their compact with God. In moral terms, acts of witness (like peace marches and civil rights demonstrations, for example) are an extension of this second religious meaning: the individual affirms by his presence his relationship to what he values.[30]

Viewed from a judicial perspective, the witness who testifies is more than an observer; to bear witness involves observation and testifying to what has been seen and to what is known:

> The presence of the witness serves to record the events being witnessed: and the witness takes responsibility, under oath and subject to penalty, for affirming the fact that the events took place. Ultimately, in legal terms, an event is not a real event unless and until the witness takes responsibility for saying it is real.[31]

Following these connotations of the testimony, imprinted in the two fields, the function of witnessing in therapy requires constant and guarded presence, observation, responsibility and mutual trust. The ability to validate and confirm the testimony is conditional on them. Seiden emphasizes the difficulty of being a witness and says:

> To be clear, the stance of witnessing is not simply the intention "to be helpful" by "finding out" . . . but a willingness to enter into the experience of the patient as a witness . . . Beyond finding out, beyond bringing insight and

order, as a consequence of those activities, the analyst-as-witness validates the importance of the person whose experience is being witnessed.[32]

Towards the end, Seiden ponders about the unique position of the function of witnessing in psychoanalytic therapy:

> My thesis, further, is that whatever else we do, or say or think we do, psycho-analysts are, above all, witnesses. We witness the internal life of our patients and in this way participate in it. I think it is the presence of the analyst-as-witness which is the primary condition under which whatever else goes on in the analysis takes place.[33]

And following that, Seiden justifies the introduction of the concept of testimony into the state of the central therapeutic functions and emphasizes its unique contribution to psychoanalysis by placing the presence of the therapist as a witness, as a link to the ancient wisdom of healing: "I am well aware that importing a term such as witness into the psychoanalytic dialogue implies, unmistakably, that the analyst takes an ethical position with respect to the life of the patient".[34]
Yet,

> At its core psychoanalysis is an ethical activity. The core matter, I suggest, is providing a presence which allows other people to make sense of their lives, to grow and to find value. To refer to this presence as bearing witness allows us to draw on ancient wisdom in understanding what such presence means – and to see psychoanalytic work in the context of centuries-old cultural experience.
>
> I suspect that the ancient religious impulse itself derives from the wish for a parental witness – for Someone or Something who knows us and cares, and in whose presence, we are less alone. I would like to think that human beings can do that for each other and that psychoanalysis is one such way.[35]

Warren Poland

Similar to Seiden, Warren Poland's discussion of testimony in therapy is not viewed solely through the prism of trauma. Poland recalls that at the beginning of his career as an analyst, the function of testimony was not considered by him to be of import, but his clinical work taught him otherwise.

In testimony, Poland sees an act facilitating understanding the otherness of the patient. In his view, the function of testimony in therapy merges concern for the wellbeing of the patient with the ability to free him: "Witnessing implies caring yet letting go".[36] The function of testimony, according to Poland, is particularly important at the end of the therapeutic process, when the patient and the therapist are on the brink of parting: "Analytic witnessing, seen most easily in the termination phase of an analysis, brings into the open of the connection between *self*-definition and the fabric of human *inter*connection."[37]

Contrary to Seiden, who claims that the act of testimony is charged with therapeutic functions from the 'Self-psychology' theory, which arises from a sense that there is a need to feel the patient's inner being, Poland emphasizes in testimony the element of separation and the recognition of the otherness of the patient: "Through witnessing, the analyst promotes the patient's burgeoning self-definition".[38] And again, unlike Seiden (and Orange), Poland separates the function of witnessing from the functions of empathy or self-object:

> witnessing may have its origin in empathic responsiveness or in offering a holding environment, but it is a function changed by maturation beyond those roots. Indeed, it reflects the patient's advancing self-other differentiation, both a growing self-definition and an increasing regard for otherness, seemingly separate processes that are intrinsically unitary.[39]

In his article "The Analytic Witnessing and Otherness" (2000), Poland concentrates on the virtues of the act of witnessing itself and outlines some technical rules for the analyst/therapist as a witness.

He states that, at the time of giving testimony, the therapist is not supposed to suggest transferential interpretations or try to progress the therapeutic process. Instead, this phase has to be one of full attention and listening in a way that gives the patient's autonomy and otherness a place of honor. Poland argues that witnessing is a respectful attention on the analyst's part, silent but active presence, a silence of engaged non intrusiveness, which demand attentive listening. That is not seeking for what can be interpreted.

Following this, Poland emphasizes the distinction between otherness and strangeness and points out that these elements are not the same, and in the therapist's position of witness, there is no element of foreignness.

In his words:

> Otherness is not synonymous with alienation; indeed, respect for otherness is the very opposite of indifference. It is acceptance, the persistence of Eros in caring for the other even in the face of Thanatos, which allows each individual to be most fully human, to facilitate growth and fullness of life in another as that person conceives them. The benefits of witnessing are thus reciprocal, enriching both patient and analyst.[40]

In terms of the therapeutic aspect, Poland views testimony as a continuation of the interpretation and sees it as external to transference. The interpretation, Poland claims, deconstructs the bond that has been built through the transferential merging. The silence of the analyst as a witness maintains this separation and contributes to the individuality of the patient:

> In witnessing, the analyst is at once both *part of* what is unfolding and *apart from* the patient's unique singularity. In witnessing, we acknowledge the genuineness

of what we grasp of the other while at the same moment acknowledging that we can never fully know or grasp what is essential in our patient's otherness. The part of a self that is, as Proust put it, "real and incommunicable" . . . – knowable but only partially knowable because of our essential otherness, the knowing and the not fully knowing both manifest in the analyst's witnessing.[41]

And about the non-verbal communication that is an integral part of the function of testimony:

The analyst's witnessing, a profound nonverbal communication of recognition, is an essential catalyst of the patient's self-realization, growing self-definition, increased knowledge of the personal self, and openness to appreciating the universe of unique others with equally valid selves – all in all, the patient's capacity for mature hate and mature love.[42]

At the end of the article, it is important for Poland to point out that all that is written doesn't in any way diminish the task of the traditional psychoanalysis:

None of this diminishes our central interpretive task of exposing and exploring unconscious meanings. An interpretation dissolves the merging implicit in transferential engagement, and the analyst's silent, respectful regard for the patient's autonomous self-analysis reinforces the patient's individuality.[43]

This present book identifies with this important viewpoint and emphasizes that the recognition of the importance of the function of testimony does not belittle the importance of other therapeutic functions but rather broadens and enriches the psychoanalytic therapeutic process.

Lewis Aron

Lewis Aron, who was the most prominent and prolific researcher of the relational school, concludes this review.

In his paper "The Transference is Indeed a Cross: Discussion of Sue Grand's 'God at an Impasse: Devotion, Social Justice, and the Psychoanalytic Subject'" (2011), Aron sees the function of testimony as a mutual act that could also be a third factor. Aron addresses the function of testimony in therapy from three main aspects:

First – he examines the outline of testimony according to the etymology of the concept and the ontology of the phenomenon.

Second – he emphasizes the importance of the concept in certain situations in which it goes beyond the act of witnessing itself.

Third – he refers to the nature of the act of testimony, of it being a risky act and of it being a value-based action.

Aron reveals that in ancient Greece, the word 'witness' meant martyr – a person who embodies his faith in his body.

He notes:

> The word Martyr derives from the Greek, for witness. We speak of "bearing witness" because witnessing is risky as it was not uncommon to be killed even crucified, for providing testimony.[44]

Aron sees testimony as an experiential and spiritual phenomenon characterized by self-sacrifice, self-inflicted suffering, which requires inner commitment and personal self-risk. He claims that history is replete with incidents in which those who gave testimony or were envoys of testimony faced being harmed and even death. Today as well, he says, journalists risk their lives in an attempt to supply testimonies from the war arena or from various natural disasters.

Another point that arises from an etymological point of view is that, in English, the phrase 'bearing witness' includes suffering in itself. That is to say that suffering is an inherent part of being a witness.

As for the etiology of giving testimony, Aron found out that the origin of the word 'testimony' is the Latin word 'testare'. He quotes Hazony:

> The word deriving from the Latin 'testare', tres, three, and stare, to stand – that is from the witness standing as a third party in litigation (Hazony, 2012, p. 51), and draws a conclusion, that the analyst as witness, providing testimony, is thus serving as "third" beyond subject and object.[45]

When Aron examines the history of the function of testimony in psychoanalysis, he points out:

> This is a new technical term in the psychoanalytic tradition as never before have analysts theorized their witnessing function. I think that this term witnessing has clearly entered our professional lexicon via trauma and Holocaust studies and derives from religious and spiritual traditions where we bear witness to God. The Bible itself is a "Testament".[46]

Aron claims that although classical psychoanalytic literature describes the therapist as an observer, in his view, the witness is much more than an observer. There are certain events or incidents in that the witness is involved, which in his absence would not take place, or without a witness, do not count as real.

For example, in legal terms, there are times when the witness is a 'third party between prosecutor and accused' and the testimony is decisive in reaching a verdict. Also "When you are witness to a wedding you are not just observing it, you participate in the creation of the marriage, and yet you are not getting married yourself."[47]

Aron believes that the therapist as a witness has to be prepared for a certain degree of sublimated and spiritualized self-sacrifice, with readiness to become vulnerable and containment of suffering. At the same time, Aron warns against pathological masochism.

In his own words:

> To bear witness as psychoanalysts requires a healthy, sublimated, spiritualized form of self-sacrifice. Not pathological masochism, but a voluntary permeability, a purposeful vulnerability, an affirmative willingness to bear some degree of suffering, and suffer their pain, to stand alongside, although separate from them, to hang with them.[48]

And he concludes:

> In my view in that what a psychoanalyst does is take in the patient's stories and form images in one's own mind about their story; the analyst symbolizes the patient's pain. It is not easy for a therapist to let the details in and transform them into one's own imagery . . . A therapist must in some significant way, experience what the patient experiences, becoming a survivor by proxy, but one who is able to symbolize the experiences of pain and even of death.[49]

List of References and Notes

1   In a footnote, that is important to our case, the translator here explains that the German word –"wirklischkeit" – indicates both reality and truth, and so it can be understood in both meanings.

2   Ferenczi, Sandor Ferenczi (1932): *The Clinical Diary*, January 31. Harvard University Press, Cambridge, MA (1995), pp. 24–25.

3   Ibid., p. 192.

4   Miller, Alice (1990): *The Untouched Key: Tracing Childhood Trauma in Creativity and Destructiveness*. Doubleday Anchor, New York, NY (1991), p. 51.

5   Ibid.

6   Herman, Lewis, Judith (1992): *Trauma and Recovery*. Basic Books, New York, NY, p. 140 & Psychiatry and Clinical Neurosciences (1998) 52 (Suppl), S145, S150.

7   Ibid.

8   Agger, Inger and Jensen, Søren Buus (1990): "Testimony as Ritual and Evidence in Psychotherapy for Political Refugees". *Journal of Traumatic Stress*, 3, pp. 115–130.

9   Ibid.

10   Herman' Judith (1992), p. 181.

11   Mollica, Richard (1988): "The Trauma Story: The Psychiatric Care of Refugee Survivors of Violence and Toture". In: *Post Traumatic Therapy and Victims of Violence* (ed. F. Osberg). Brunner/Mazel, New York, pp. 295–314.

12   Felman, Shoshana and Laub, Dori (1992): *Testimony: The Crisis of Witnessing in Literature, Psychoanalysis and History*. Routledge, London, Great Britan; Taylor and Francis, New York, p. 180.

13   Ibid., p. 5.

14   Orange, Donna M. (1995): *Emotional Understanding: Studies in Psychoanalytic Epistemology*. New York and London, p. 135.

15   Ibid., p. 136.

16   Ibid., p. 139.

17 Ibid., p. 137.
18 Ibid., p. 140.
19 Ibid.
20 Orange, M. Donna (2011): *The Suffering Stranger: Hermeneutics For Everyday Clinical Practice*. Routledge/Taylor & Francis, New York, NY, p. 9.
21 Ibid., p. 38.
22 Margalit, Avishai (2002): *The Ethics of Memory*. Harvard University Press, Cambridge, MA, in Orange M. Donna (2011).
23 Orange (2011).
24 Seiden, M. Henry (1996): "The Healing Presence: Part I: The Witness as Self-Object Function". *Psychoanalytic Review*, 83, pp. 685–693.
25 Among Heinz Kohut's important contributions to the psychoanalytic dialogue has been the concept of 'self-object': another person (originally, a parent) whose presence is sufficiently internalized that that presence is experienced as part of the self. A self-object completes, stabilizes, soothes and otherwise integrates the experience of self.
26 Seiden (1996), p. 691.
27 Ibid., pp. 684–685.
28 Ibid., p. 686.
29 Ibid., p. 690.
30 Ibid., p. 685.
31 Ibid.
32 Ibid., p. 691.
33 Ibid., p. 686.
34 Ibid., p. 691.
35 Ibid., pp. 691–692.
36 Poland, Warren (2000): "The Analyst's Witnessing and Otherness". *Journal of American Association*, 48, pp. 17–34, 32.
37 Ibid., p. 17.
38 Ibid., p. 31.
39 Ibid., p. 17.
40 Ibid., p. 32.
41 Ibid., p. 32–33.
42 Ibid., p. 32.
43 Ibid.
44 Lewis, Aron (2011): "A Commentary to Sue Grand's Paper: God at an Impasse". Unpublished manuscript, and in: "The Transference is Indeed a Cross". *Psychoanalytic Dialogues*, 23 (2013), pp. 464–474. Taylor & Francis, Routledge Group, UK.
45 Ibid., pp. 19–20.
46 Ibid., p. 19.
47 Ibid., p. 20.
48 Ibid., p. 22.
49 Ibid.

Chapter 12

A Unique Kind of Patient's Testimony in the Therapeutic Process

Zipi Rosenberg Schipper

Introduction

Unlike the the analyst/therapist's position as a witness that lasts throughout the therapeutic process, there is special testimony for which the analyst/therapist is required to participate in a different kind of witnessing. This kind of testimony, which is given by patients, appears just once or occupies a number of sessions. This refers to a patient's testimony which is almost always exceptional in its nature, meaning it is divergent in its content from the ongoing therapeutic text.

This chapter concentrates on these testimonies.

During treatment, there is a moment when a patient gives testimony of a piece of life that he kept to himself, and in most cases, he does not want to work it through or even mention it again.

These are bits of life which, in most cases, the treatment room is the only place in which they 'come into the light', and they are woven into the therapeutic space, not as a metaphor of the patient's inner world, but as an event that happened in reality and the need to share it with the therapist transcends any strong inhibition the patient may feel.

The range of those testimonies is wide. There are life stories that have been 'hidden': personal secrets, family secrets, forbidden loves, painful experiences, or shameful acts (Orange 1995), reflections, thoughts of revenge (Ullman 2006), as well as experiences of success and achievements to which there are no witnesses and as a result of which they did not gain recognition.

Common to them all is that they are real experiences in the life of the patient. Almost always, such testimonies are given when the other person, who was a partner or knew about the secret, dies, and it becomes too heavy a burden to carry on one's own. These testimonies are delivered only when **trust** has been established in the relationship and an atmosphere of 'being at home' has been created. Its delivery creates a fragile situation that can be very easily disturbed or stopped. In other words, when the patient sees the treatment room as a **safe place** and knows that the therapist will listen to him and believe him and not be judgmental.

Such spoken testimony is another territory of space and time within the therapeutic dialog, or in Wittgenstein's (1953, 1994) formulation – another

DOI: 10.4324/9781003403920-14

"language game" (sprachspiel).[1] It has its own 'grammar' and its own rhythm. The therapist as recipient follows a different set of rules that differs from that which is generally accepted. While the testimony is being given, the 'one who knows' is the patient and not the therapist. The therapist as witness yields his sovereignty, a move that creates a state of mutual giving and, as a result, a change in dialectics.

The patient's testimony has recently been considered a good exploratory tool for the therapeutic process. However, in most cases, it is a material that was intended to be only a testimony and should remain as a testimony. Patients seek not to treat this material in an interpretive way nor to apply analytical intervention to it.

Moreover, this particular testimony was said in order to be said and should remain as raw material. It is almost always the case that the patient delivers the testimony because he is alone in the story and out of a desire to have the therapist be his witness. The therapist who is interested in working through the given testimony, or even raising the matter again, has to ask the patient for permission.

Being captive to the traditional psychoanalytic concept, the usual discourse among therapists upon hearing the testimonies of patients focuses on analyzing the space occupied by the testimony in the patient's life rather than being a witness to his testimony. Such discussion misses the unique contribution of the act of testimony itself.

A Short Vignette Will Illustrate This Claim

A patient in her sixties told me after about six months of therapy:

> When I was young, I did a terrible thing.
> It's not easy for me to tell you about, so I'll just say it quickly.
> My brother and I succeeded to escape from the ghetto, where our whole family was. We joined a group of people that were hiding in the woods. One day, as we were gathering potatoes in the field, we saw a man staring at us, standing on the way to the forest. We threw away the potatoes we gathered and approached him. He started to ask questions: "Who we are?", "Where are our friends hiding?" We were afraid; we knew that he was going to hand us and the whole group over to the Germans. It was him or us; we punched him and killed him.
> I don't regret it; we saved ourselves and the whole group.

Then she added:

> Neither of us told anyone about it, not to our spouses nor to our children. As long as my brother was alive, it didn't bother me so much. But last year, he died, and I have been left alone with this secret, which became too much a burden for me to bear.

The treatment continued for about six more years after that, but we never returned to this story.

List of References and Note

1 Wittgenstein, Ludwig (1953): *Philosophical Investigations*. Blackwell Publishing, London, England, # 23, p. 4.

Chapter 13

Summary of the Main Characteristics of the Therapist as a Witness and the Patient's Testimony

Zipi Rosenberg Schipper

Introduction

Testimony delivered in analytic therapy is personal testimony, which is more a matter of an action than of a theory and indeed, the concept has never been analyzed theoretically.

The attempt here is to conceptualize the function of testimony and witnessing in philosophical terms and with psychological tools by indicating technical rules for it in clinical practice.

The purpose is to try to bridge the gap that has been created in the space between the clinical work and the psychoanalytic theory regarding the status of the function of witnessing in therapy. And, no less importantly, the gap that has recently emerged between the increasing interest in the discourse of testimony in psychoanalysis and the psychoanalytic inattention to the virtues of the act of testimony itself.

This is the first endeavor – ever – to conceptualize the phenomenon of spoken testimony in therapy, and it is conducted on two levels: the clinical and the technical.

The summary refers first to the standing of the analyst/therapist as a witness, followed by the way in which it relates to the analysand/patient's testimony.

Lines Characterizing the Position of the Analyst/Therapist as a Witness

The stand of the analyst/therapist as a witness is a distinct function in analytic therapy. It is in the background at all times throughout the therapeutic process. In Seiden's view (1996), it constitutes "the primary condition under which whatever else goes on, in the analysis."[1]

As said, there are psychoanalysts who see its main importance in the first stages of therapeutic analysis when trust and confidence are gained (Orange 1995), and there are those who view its importance during the termination phase, when the need to recognize the otherness of the patient arises (Poland 2000).

DOI: 10.4324/9781003403920-15

Chana Ullman's (2006) words are especially relevant here:

> In witnessing the listening is not neutral but takes sides to allow for the evolvement of alternative forms of self-experience . . . The uniqueness of the process of testimony lies in the fact that the therapist is 'an-other' . . . The testimony is a specific function of the analyst who liberates the patient's concealed story and facilitates validation of the subjective external reality . . . Testimony is a curative element . . . Witnessing consists of the presence of a therapist who neither looks for efficacy nor tries to interpret the patient's story.[2]

The presence, trust and listening of the therapist as a witness who recognizes the patient's external reality and accepts the details conveyed as they are, create a validation of worth.

To be a witness entails verbal and non-verbal communication of recognition and validation. The act resembles Gadamer's description (Gadamer 2004)

> Once again we discover that the person who is understanding, does not know and judge as one who stands apart and unaffected, but rather he thinks along with the other from the perspective of a specific bond of belonging, as if he too were affected[3]

The stance of listening is not easy for the traditional analytic therapist, whose approach is based on interpretive intervention. Moreover, it is given that in the treatment room, it is the therapist who 'knows' (besserwiser) (Orange 2010). In being a witness, the therapist must withdraw from his 'knowing sovereignty' and accept that at this moment in time, it is the patient who 'knows'. This is a significant point in the therapeutic process, which is not at all obvious and means the reduction of the therapist's sovereign position during that situation.

The key words of the stance of the therapist are, therefore: being present, listening, trusting, being with and mutuality.

Martin Buber, in his book "*I and Thou*" (1923), relates almost exactly in these words to the essentiality of mutual testimony in the act of therapy:

> If a genuine psychotherapist is satisfied to "analyze" his patient . . . he may successfully accomplish some repairs. At best, he may help a diffuse soul that is poor in structure to achieve at least some concentration and order. But he cannot absolve his true task, which is the regeneration of a stunted personal center. That can be brought off only by a man who grasps with the profound eye of a physician the buried, latent unity of the suffering soul . . . the therapist . . . must stand not only at his own pole of the bipolar relationship but also at the other pole, experiencing the effects of his own actions.[4]

Guidelines for the Therapist as Witness

There are a number of significant references to the analyst/therapist as a witness that have appeared in the psychoanalytic review. Some are theoretical thoughts, and some are technical rules. The majority of the recommendations for the therapist as a witness summarized here are based on those references.

- As analysts, "whatever else we do, or say, or think we do, psychoanalysts are, above all, witnesses."[5]
- "Psychoanalysts, like any other witness, is a player of a cognitive, emotional, spiritual and ethical kind in what is witnessed – giving the experience its reality, and validating thoughts, feelings and judgments".[6]
- "Witnessing, a special form of participation in the intersubjective field, makes the other's experience real and valid."[7]
- Witnessing "is what Kohut intended by his term 'empathy'. With the passage of time the understanding and definition of this concept became blurred and it is the concern of the therapist that is one of the foundation stones of witnessing".[8]
- "The absence of witnesses in the course of a person's life, leads to developmental problems and difficult situations of loneliness".[9]
- It is up to the therapist as a witness to act without presumptions (Orange 2001).
- "Testimony is one of the forms of emotional availability which the analyst must embrace. The patient, in other words, can experience raw pain, but needs the responsive other to construe it, to understand its enormity and meaning. Analyst and patient make sense of it together".[10]
- "The analyst as a witness, by knowing and by taking responsibility for that knowledge, participates in a psychological way in the experience being witnessed. We witness the internal life of our patients and in this way participate in it."[11]
- "It is the presence of the analyst-as-witness which is the primary condition under which whatever else goes on in the analysis takes place."[12]
- The presence of a witness is a necessary condition of growth and is productive of the integration of self at every level of development. The absence is a painful state which threatens the cohesion of self (Orange 1995, Seiden 1996).
- Psychoanalysts are, above all, witnesses.[13]
- "On closer examination it turns out in every case that a particular witness helped the child experience his feelings."[14]
- "The presence of the analyst enables the child to experience what is happening to him and the adult, who had been this child to know what happened to him."[15]
- "At its core psychoanalysis is an ethical activity. The core matter . . . is providing a presence which allows other people to make sense of their lives, to grow and to find value. To refer to this presence as bearing witness allows us to draw on ancient wisdom in understanding what such presence means – and to see psychoanalytic work in the context of centuries-old cultural experience."[16]

- "To make sense of things, whether outer or inner, to bring order, reality, and value requires the responsible presence of others, that is, requires the presence of witnesses."[17]
- "Parents, and friends and lovers, and psychoanalysts, are self-objects. They are also witnesses. They see, record, name, validate, care about and take responsibility for what they witness".[18]
- "I suspect that the ancient religious impulse itself derives from the wish for a parental witness – for Someone or Something who knows us and cares, and in whose presence we are less alone. I would like to think that human beings can do that for each other and that psychoanalysis is one such way."[19]
- The interpretation of testimony is of 'hermeneutic of trust' (Orange 2010).
- The therapist as a witness is able to call things by name. Naming provides validation and creates a different standing of the testimony for the patient. It is a position that is easier to bear (Orange 2011).
- Frequently, what analysts "call denial, disavowal or unconsciousness, may often be an experience never truly experienced, because of the absence of a witness in his life at that time. In such cases, one has to be both a believing as well as a protective witness."[20]
- The existence of testimony in therapy is dependent on a believing therapist who forgoes the ethic of 'sovereign' and establishes 'an ethic of presence' (Sagi 2011).
- "Close listening is in itself an important form of interpretation . . . and fully deserves to be considered psychoanalytic."[21]
- Witnessing undoes dissociation and allows a person to establish the continuity of a self-possessed life. It undoes shame and restores the positive valuation of the self.
- Field work requires constant decisions. One of them is to illuminate an issue spoken by the patient and work it through. Sometimes making such a choice is not easy, and a pause becomes necessary. In order to resist a therapist's premature application of theoretical knowledge and preconceived ideas about them, a "period of hesitation" (Winnicott 1958: 53)[22] is necessary. Without the space created by this hesitation, there can be no room for analytic discovery or play. The function of testimony allows both therapist and patient such a "period of hesitation" (Casement 1985, p. 295)[23] by maintaining the possibilities until one makes itself prominent,
- In light of the current trend to lessen dichotomies, there is a call among psychoanalysts to encourage mutual situations. By its very nature, psychoanalysis cannot be entirely mutual (Buber 1959, Aron 2013) because of the asymmetry that has to be preserved. However, testimony as a distinct function can do so because, in its essence, it is a reciprocal phenomenon and is perhaps the only mutual space in which the patient meets the therapist as subject, and the therapist meets the patient as subject
- Psychoanalysis moves between opposing world views, and there is a fundamental tension between them (Wilson 2003).[24] The position of the therapist as

a witness offers a way of holding on to both ends and possibly even merging them. One can relate to it as containing two images of a worldview displayed in parallel on one screen.

Characteristics of the Patient's Testimony: Every Person Wants His Voice to Be Heard

As said, in the psychoanalytic discourse on testimony, there are very few, and poorly designed, references to the testimony of a patient. Consequently, all the characteristics summarized here in this context were learned through my clinical work.

- The patient offers his testimony only when full trust has been attained between the patient and the therapist and an atmosphere of 'being at home' has been created.
- At the time when a patient delivers her/his testimony, the heart of the act is the given testimony and not the encounter between the patient and therapist.
- While the testimony is delivered, the 'one who knows' ("besserwiser", Orange 2011) is the patient and not the therapist. This differs from what is commonly accepted in the traditional psychoanalytic process.
- The testimony of a patient is accepted as is.
- While a testimony is delivered, there is a different mutual giveness (Spielberg 1948).
- Although the testimony of a patient is revealed as being a good exploratory tool, regarding the different kinds of testimony, in most cases, patients are not interested in working through the material and prefer to leave it as unprocessed raw material.

Summary of the Two Functions of Testimony in Therapy

Between therapist and patient, where the therapist as witness believes the patient's testimony exists in the background, in parallel to the specific content that arises. In such cases, the ability for validation, recognition and healing is expressed by the patient's knowing that the listening therapist believes him and trusts his feelings, his memories and the words he chooses to use. And there are moments when the testimony turns from being a background to a shape. That is to say, the therapeutic dyad becomes a witness of a witness, and these are the 'pure' moments of testimony and witnessing.

List of References and Notes

1 Seiden, M. Henry (1996): "The Healing Presence: Part I: The Witness as Self-Object Function". *Psychoanalytic Review*, 83, pp. 685–693, 686.
2 Chana, Ullman (2006): "Bearing Witness: Across the Barriers in Society and in the Clinic", *Psychoanalytic Dialogs*, 16, pp. 181–198, 194.
3 Gadamer, H. G. (2004): *Truth and Method*. Contiuum Publishing Group, London and New York, NY (1975), p. 332.

4   Buber Martin (1923): *I and Thou*, Translated into English. Scribner Classics Martino Publishing, Eastford, CT (1937), pp. 178–179, 158.
5   Ibid.
6   Seiden (1996), p. 685.
7   Orange, Dona M. (1995): *Emotional Understanding: Studies in Psychoanalytic Epistemology*. The Guilford Press, New York and London, p. 140.
8   Seiden (1966), p. 691.
9   Ibid., p. 686.
10   Orange (1995), p. 140.
11   Seiden (1996), p. 685.
12   Ibid., p. 686.
13   Ibid.
14   Miller, Alice (1991): *The Untouched Key: Tracing Childhood Trauma in Creativity and Destructiveness*. Doubleday Anchor, New York, 1991, pp. 50–51.
15   Orange (1995), p. 139.
16   Ibid., pp. 691–692.
17   Ibid., p. 692.
18   Seiden (1996), p. 688.
19   Ibid., p. 692.
20   Orange (1995), p. 137.
21   Orange, Donna M. (2010): *Thinking for Clinicians*. Routledge, New York, NY, p. 115.
22   Winnicott, Donald W. (1958): *Collected Papers: Through Pediatrics to Psychoanalysis*. Tavistock, London, England.
23   Casement, Patric (1985): *On Learning from the Patient*. Guilford Press, New York and London (1990), p. 295.
24   Wilson, Arnold (2003): "Ghosts of Paradigms Past: The Once and Future Evolution of Psychoanalytic Thought". *Journal of the American Psychoanalytic Association*, 51, pp. 825–855.

Chapter 14

Why Testimony and Why Now?

Zipi Rosenberg Schipper

Introduction

This chapter makes use of the review of the psychoanalytic literature and the philo-sophical debates referred to, throughout the book in order to answer the question: "Why testimony and why now?"

As said, testimony in therapy and the extent of its authenticity doesn't have its own theoretical anchor. This lack of a specific theoretical base is what makes the function of testimony unique in the therapeutic framework. Paradoxically this is both its weakness and its strength.

The weakness is expressed by the fact that for testimony in therapy, there is no psychoanalytic theory that advances its status in the therapeutic field, and it forges its way via its internal strength. And its strength, which stems from the same source, finds its expression via the idea that non-belongingness enables the act of testimony to serve as an intermediary space or as a 'third' force, since whatever is not linked to a specific anchor can move between modes of being that are poles apart.

Over the last decade of the 20th century, the psychoanalytic discourse has shown an increasing interest in the dialogic philosophers, who were active throughout the century. These include Martin Buber, Hans-Georg Gadamer, Ludwig Wittgen-stein, Emmanuel Levinas and others, whose doctrines supported dialectic relations, mutuality and situations of dialogue (Orange 2010). Equally influential, and per-haps more so, was the postmodern stream of thought in that it was the dominant force in erasing absolute conventionally accepted concepts and challenging polari-zation. Moreover, postmodernism had a significant impact on the Intersubjective and the Relational psychoanalytic schools (Aron 1996, Orange 1995, Benjamin 1998 and others) and created an environment that encouraged moderation of psy-choanalytical dichotomies such as object and subject, or inner and external reality. These, too, turn ideological non-belongingness into an actual advantage.

Opposing Worldviews Star the Psychoanalytic Thinking

Freud chose to present the psychoanalytic model as scientific, which, at the time, relied on the positivist worldview. His working assumption was that a worldview

DOI: 10.4324/9781003403920-16

(*weltanschauung*) "is an intellectual construction which solves all the problems of our existence uniformly, on the basis of one overriding hypothesis."[1]

But in Freud's clinical practice, there was not a "uniform solution", and in many cases, his approach contradicted the outlines of the theory that he himself had advanced. His writings also included texts that were not in line with scientific principles. Consequently, a dialectic tension was created, which didn't really disturb Freud, who was at ease with it, but did disturb his followers. This conceptual tension between opposites that every time adopted different guises exists in psychoanalysis to this day.[2]

Arnold Wilson (2003)[2] dealt with this tension and its impact on the molding and construction of approaches in great detail. Wilson claimed that two opposing world views historically molded and altered the psychoanalytic theories and that every one of the hypotheses is an axis around which a therapist works.

According to Wilson, the way in which psychoanalytic doctrine moves between hypotheses involves one theory focusing on the intrapsychic conflict – whilst the other approach works on interpersonal internalization.

In his own words:

> An example of the psychoanalytic mode of thought is put forward concerning how psychoanalytic theories have historically been constituted and transformed. The model of world hypotheses, characterized by multiple irresolvable truth claims, captures the nature of most psychoanalytic theorizing until about 1970. Each of two world hypotheses – one grounded in intrapsychic conflict (seen when the analyst observes from outside the transference) and the other in interpersonal internalization (seen when the analyst observes from inside the bidirectional interactive processes) – is an autonomous and self-sufficient aggregate.[3]

These conflicting approaches were already evident in the differences of view between Freud and Ferenczi and later on between Winnicott and Kohut. More precisely, the differences were mostly evident in the alternative views expressed by the "Object-relations" school and "Self-psychology", as well as between "Ego-Psychology" and "Self-psychology".[4]

Lewis Aron referred to this in his book (1996):

- "One of the most important axis along which to organize the traditional psychoanalytic method, is the unilateral extracting information from the patient . . . this axis is based on the assumption that the analyst has sufficient ability of an autonomous observing ego."[5]
- And the opposite approach: "Here analysts are inevitably sucked for ongoing realizations in action with patients . . .and thus will not be able to maintain an adequate degree of disconnection."[6]

In this last approach, noted by Steven Mitchell (2004), which is nowadays the accepted approach in most psychoanalytic schools, there is a certain lack of distinction between the therapist and patient. The therapist is part of the transferential process and acts out of it.[7]

The clear distinction between the two approaches is in the kind of relations created between the patient and the therapist.

At the beginning, psychoanalytic work focused on the patient's inner psychic space, whilst the therapist was external to the transference process and distinct from it (as Freud thought, at least until the 1930s).[8] The perception of the "unconscious" that was accepted at the time and the Cartesian thinking that was dominant then in the philosophical world supported this.

And another opinion: Hoffman (1998) dealt with this ideological tension, talking about two main ideologies Crossing psychoanalysis, but his approach to both was different from Wilson's. According to him, in both approaches, the therapist must reduce himself – each time to a different position – "And always to be able to put himself in the patient's place."[9]

Testimony in Therapy as an Intermediary Space That Moves Between Opposing World Views

The review of psychoanalytic writing, cited above, further emphasizes the lack of the theoretical anchor of the function of testimony in therapy. Every therapeutic approach that refers to testimony has done so using terminology that reflects its worldview. And every researcher who has written about testimony has done so in line with his own professional tendency. Thus, the evaluation and recognition of the positioning of testimony and witnessing in therapy varies, depending on which of the main therapeutic approaches is under discussion. And so, the function of testimony is not to be found solely in either one of the dominant psychoanalytic approaches but rather in the psychoanalytic space between them. This paragraph enumerates the virtues of testimony, being in an intermediate space and a therapeutic function that is not dependent on theoretical basis.

The researchers Seiden (1996) and Poland (2000) – who are amongst the most dominant in the investigation of the function of testimony in therapy – describe its role in therapy from opposing points of view.

In the act of witnessing, Seiden sees the main and essential aspect of the function of 'self-object' and of the function of 'empathy'.[10] Both are attributable to 'self-psychology', which is characterized by touching or reaching out for the patient's inner world.

Poland, on the other hand, emphasizes the power of witnessing to recognize the 'otherness' of the patient, meaning that the therapist as witness remains external to the transferential process. Poland describes testimony as the continuation of the function of interpretation, and according to him, the interpretation dismantles the bond evident in the transferential integration, and the silence of the analyst as witness encourages this separation. His famous statement is, "In witnessing, the analyst is at once part of what is unfolding and apart from the patient's singularity".[11]

The juxtaposition of the studies of Seiden and Poland shows that in the act of witnessing, there is a line of fusion and feeling from within, as well as an ability to separate.

The combination of these two aspects is necessary for the healing process because for testimony to have a therapeutic effect, it must include both an internal and an external position. That is to say, the act of testimony in therapy needs a present and observing therapist who is not judgmental and allows the testimony to come into being. At the same time, the act of testimony becomes futile if the patient feels that the therapist remains 'external' and is not part of the situation.

The Element of Mutuality in Testimony in Psychoanalytic Therapy

The aspect of mutuality, which is a dominant component of personal testimony, reinforces the idea of placing the act of testimony in intermediate spaces. In the former discussion of whether personal testimony is dialogic or a monologist – it seems that on the continuum between them, the act of testimony, due to its inherent reciprocity, is much closer to a dialogue than to a monologue.

Dialogue has a mutual influence on both participants, as does the act of listening to a given testimony. The person who listens and understands does not stand apart and does not remain unaffected, as Hans Georg Gadamer notes:

> To reach an understanding in a dialogue is not matter of putting oneself forward . . . but being transformed into a communion in which we do not remain what we were."[12] . . . "Openness to the other, then involves recognizing that I myself must accept some things that are against me even though no one else forces me to do so.[13]

Testimony in treatment is mutual in that the therapist as a witness is listening to and believing in the patient's testimony. This way, he becomes a witness to a witness. This mode is reinforced by Lewis Aron's (1996) description of the concept of mutuality: "By mutual I mean that there is bidirectional influence between patient and analyst"[14] . . . "Mutuality refers to a situation in which one experiences an event both from one's own and from the other's perspective."[15]

In his book "*I and Thou*" (1923), Martin Buber talked about mutuality in therapy and argues that it is appropriate for psychotherapeutic treatment to be reciprocal but not to be symmetrical:

> Another, no less instructive example of the normative limits of mutuality may be found in the relationship between a genuine psychotherapist and his patient, . . . In the presence of the therapist the unwell individual gains mutuality, acceptance and communication . . . However the unique quality of this bond, is that the attachment to the 'healer' would end as soon as the patient decided to practice

the art of embracing and actually succeeded in experiencing events also from the doctor's point of view.[16]

In his attempt to distinguish the many dimensions of mutuality in the therapeutic relationship, Aron found Buber's work useful. He notes:

> Like many analysts who have loosely used the word mutuality, Buber did not consider its diverse meanings and implications. On one hand, Buber suggested that teachers help students. And therapists help patients to become whole person by engaging them in I-You relations. On the other hand, he suggested that therapists and teachers maintain their distance. In my view, what Buber was objecting to in arguing that psychotherapy could not be fully mutual is more clearly stated by noting the inevitable asymmetry in the relationship, the difference in roles and responsibilities between patient and therapist.[17]

Buber (1923) also tried, in his way, to distinguish between reciprocity and mutuality and argued that reciprocity refers to any situation in which each being acts on the other.

Aron (1996) did not completely agree with this definition and formulated it differently, noting that: "Reciprocity seems closer to what I have referred mutuality of regulation, or mutuality of influence, where what Buber terms mutuality I have referred to as mutuality of recognition."[18]

Ogden's view of mutuality and its contribution to psychoanalysis are relevant here:

> The creation of a mutual creative space allows both psychotherapist and patient to play with the idea of being the other. In this process, the "other" helps create, crystallize, and sharpen the identity of both participants in the encounter. As a result, both may experience personal growth. Playing the other enriches and expands the boundaries of the person/self while, at the same time, strengthening them by sharpening the differences between them.[19]

As Winnicott put it:

> The mother creates the infant and the infant creates the mother.[20]

In addition, there is another topical advantage of mutuality, emphasized by Aron (1996), that also relates to testimony and to its unique contribution to the psychoanalytic therapeutic process.

> One further dimension of mutuality that has generally gone unnoticed, is the way in which both patient and analyst mutually contribute to the development of psychoanalytic theory and practice.[21]

From all of the above, it can be said that the motif of mutuality of personal testimony adds an important dimension and expands the boundaries, and in being part of the therapeutic process, it constitutes a mutual space (perhaps the only one, as said) in which therapist and patient meet as subjects.

The two aspects – the absence of a theoretical base and the motif of mutuality – insert testimony in intermediate space and allow it to move between contrasting ideologies and even to try to bridge between them, emphasizing its special value in light of the consolidation of the tendency to minimize binary states and increasingly rely on situations of mutuality.

Intermediary Spaces and a Third in Coping With Polarization

A number of researchers paid attention to the advantage of a therapeutic position that doesn't belong to a specific worldview and can serve as an intermediary factor or as a 'third'. These include Bass (1998), who posited that "Holding a certain worldview (*weltenschtauung*) can harm the analysis."[22]

As a rule, any model built on two pillars is not a stable structure and needs a third force to 'strengthen' its base. All the more so, a theoretical model related to human behavior, which is never fully anticipated. Freud understood this principle, and in building the two primary models of the psychoanalytic theory – the topographical model: the conscious, the preconscious and the unconscious (originally published in Freud's "Interpretation of Dreams", 1899); and the structural model: Ego, Super Ego and Id (Published in this name in 1920) – he made sure to base them on a triangular structure.

In this context, there are also commentators who attribute to the therapeutic 'setting' a sort of testimony of place and time, which could also function as a third entity in the sense that it is a 'holding' force that is beyond the therapist and the patient.

In Aron's view, Freud was a person of many contradictions, as is his theory. Aron believes that this positioned Freud in an intermediary area, and in this context, Aron, who was influenced by Postmodernism, attributes to the intermediary area the ability to contain contradictions and the power to create a new world.

In his struggles with binary situations, Aron was careful not to cancel anything but rather to use the ideas to bridge between conflicting modes and to recognize the value of mutual situations. In his book "*A Meeting of Minds*" (1996), Aron develops the element of mutuality in almost every area of psychoanalysis and claims that a multiplicity of mutual situations are a key to bridging between ideological poles.[23]

According to Aron, escaping from the restrictiveness of the binary modes, "which characterizes psychoanalysis in almost every sense and every dimension and flattens it."[24] makes it appropriate that it be replaced by a mutual space with the patient (though not symmetrically), and that in such a way forms will be found of a 'third' space that will hold the situation.

He notes:

> Thus, the Relational approach is an attempt to bridge theories that have tra-
> ditionally emphasized either internal object relations or external interpersonal
> relations, the intrapsychic or the interpersonal, constitutional factors or environ-
> mental factors, one-person psychology versus two-person psychologies.[25]

Jessica Benjamin (2004), who is also influenced by the Postmodern and Decon-
structive ideology, alongside the great influence of Hegel's ideas on her, especially
the "*Master and Slave dialectics*" (1977),[26] describes psychoanalysis's need to
escape from the splits of master and slave. According to Benjamin, one has to
aspire to the 'third' factor in the form of equality between the ruler and the subject.
It is required for the conflictual space between the patient and the therapist, maintaining both the connection between them and their separateness.[27]

Which Third Can Fulfill the Function of Testimony

Winnicott's work (1971) moved the focus of the therapeutic arena from the patient
to the intermediary space and named it "potential space".[28] This is a space in which
there is a movement between the therapist and the patient, as well as a movement
within the person – between his inner reality and the external reality. Since then,
psychoanalysts have begun to pay attention to intermediary spaces.

In Winnicott's words, "There is a need for this third part in a person which is
the intermediary zone of the experience to which both the internal reality and the
external reality contribute."[29]

Stephen Mitchell (1991) carried on this direction and expressed the need to
change some paradigms of thought and to indicate the psychoanalytic need for a
'third'. Mitchell argued that we are stuck between two binary worlds of the vulnerable and the non-vulnerable, of ruler and ruled, and that the only way of escaping
from this is in adding a 'third' to the therapeutic situation.

Following Mitchel, Aron (1996), in an effort to terminate some of the hierarchy, combined the concepts of intermediary space and 'third' and formed a third
alternative. It was Aron who discerned that the act of testimony was 'qualified'
to be a 'third'. As he investigated the etymology of the word 'testimony' and
found its linguistic sources in Latin, he discovered that the linguistic definition
of 'testimony' is 'third' (testare, three).[30] Also, as mentioned, the witness has a
role of a 'third' in a marriage ceremony and as a 'third' between prosecutor and
defendant.

The self-evident conclusion is that coping well with the polarized worldviews
is in intermediary spaces, and a third factor that makes possible an ambivalent
tentative pause. In situations of ambiguity, intermediary spaces offer containment
from an emotional and cognitive point of view. All of these aspects characterize the
phenomenon of personal testimony.

List of References and Notes

1 Freud, Sigmond (1933): "New Introductory Lectures on Psychoanalysis". *S.E.*, 22, p. 120.

2 Wilson, Arnold (2003): "Ghosts of Paradigms Past: The Once and Future Evolution of Psychoanalytic Thought". *Journal of the American Psychoanalytic Association*, 51, pp. 825–855.

3 Ibid., p. 824.

4 Ibid., p. 826.

5 Aron, Lewis (1996): *Meeting of Minds: Mutuality in Psychoanalysis*. Analytic Press Incorporation, Burlingame, CA, p. 161.

6 Ibid., 162.

7 Stephen A. Mitchell and Black, Margaret J. (1966): *Freud and Beyond: A History of Modern Psychoanalytic Thought*. Basic Books Publishing, New York, NY.

8 Mitchell, Steven (1988): *Relational Concepts in Psychoanalysis*. Harvard University Press. Cambridge, MA.

9 Hoffman, Irwin Z. Hoffman (1998): *Ritual and Spontaneity in the Psychoanalytic Process*. The Analytic Press, Hillsdale, NJ.
   The term 'selfobject', which Seiden uses, appears in his article unhyphenated. Aner Govrin comments on the removal of the hyphen, which separated between the self and the object, between inner and outer and between objectivity and subjectivity, and expresses an additional from classical psychoanalysis release. (2004), p. 120 (Hebrew).

10 Seiden, Henry (1966): The Healing Presence: Part I: The Witness as Self-Object Function". *Psychoanalytic Review*, 83 (1996), pp. 685–693, 686.

11 Poland, Warren (2000): "The Analyst's Witnessing and Otherness". *Journal of American Association*, 48, pp. 17–34, 163.

12 Gadamer, Hans Georg (2004): *Truth and Method*. Contiuum Publishing Group, London and New York, p. 355.

13 Lewis, Aron (1996): *A Meeting of Minds: Mutuality in Psychoanalysis*. Analytic Press, Inc., Burlingame, CA, p. 371.

14 Ibid., p. 149.

15 Aron, Lewis (1996): *A Meeting of Minds: Mutuality in Psychoanalysis*. Analytic Press, Inc. Burlingame, CA, p. 156.

16 Buber, Martin (1923): *I and Thou*. Charles Scribner's Sons, New York, NY (1970), pp. 177–178.

17 Aron, Lewis (1996), p. 157.

18 Ibid., p. 156.

19 Ogden, Thomas H. (1986): "The Matrix of the Mind: Object Relations and the Psychoanalytic Dialogue." *International Journal of Psychoanalysis*, 66, 129–141, Taylor & Francis, Routledge Group. UK.

20 Winnicott, Donald Woods (1971): *Playing and Reality*. Basic Books, New York. U.S.A

21 Ibid., p. 158.

22 Bass, Alan (1998): "Sigmund Freud: The Questions of a Weltanschauung and of Defense". In: *Psychoanalytic Versions of the Human Condition: Philosophies of Life and Their Impact on Practice* (ed. Paul Marcus and Alan Rosenberg). New York University Press, New York, pp. 412–446, 424.

23 Aron (1996), p. 137.

24 Ibid., 102.

25 Ibid., p. 861.

26 Hegel, Georg Wilhelm Friedrich (1967): *The Phenomenology of the Mind, the Master and the Slave* #199, p. 523, ASIN: B00416287M. Harper Colophon Publishing, New York, NY.

27 Benjamin, Jessica (2004): "Beyond Doer and Done to: An Intersubjective View of Thirdness". *Psychoanalysis Quarterly*, 73, pp. 5–46.

28 Donald Woods Winnicott defined his concept of "potential space" as follows: "I refer to the hypothetical area that exists (but cannot exist) between the baby and the object (mother or part of mother) during the phase of the repudiation of the object as not-me, that is, at the end of being merged in with the object." Donald Woods Winnicott (1971), p. 107.

29 Winnicott, Donald Woods (1999): *Playing and Reality*. Basic Books, New York, NY, p. 396.

30 Aron, Lewis (2013): "The Transference Is Indeed a Cross". *Psychoanalytic Dialogues, The International Journal of Relational Perspectives*, 23, pp. 464–474.

Chapter 15

Two Comments, Possible Criticism and Epilogue

Zipi Rosenberg Schipper

Two Important Comments

This book does not at all deny the traditional principles of psychoanalysis and certainly does not attempt to change the therapeutic situation. Rather, it seeks to take advantage of the space that has opened up at the crossroads in which psychoanalysis finds itself and hopefully to establish the recognition of a function that is essential to therapeutic work, irrespectively of the contests that arise in any given therapeutic situation.

Furthermore, it has to be stressed that testimony in therapy is a distinct and basic therapeutic function in all the psychoanalytic schools of thought. This epistemic and ethical recognition is not a breach of the rules, but rather fills a lack in the psychoanalytic form in all its ideological varieties. The time has come for this function to have a central place in the list of therapeutic functions, and as Orange says: "Better late than never".[1]

The Second Comment is in fact a question: What will be considered a psychoanalytic treatment?

Would it be a therapy throughout which the therapist serves as a witness who is being present and attentive to the patient?

One in which the patient experiences every interpretive intervention by the therapist as a disturbance of experiential continuity that develops within him – as in the therapy described in the prologue? Will that not be considered psychoanalytic therapy?

In order to try and answer this question, I return to Freud.

In the first Encyclopedic chapter[2] Freud outlined four essential conscious foundations for psychoanalytic therapy.

- Recognition of unconscious mental processes in a person.
- Recognition of the theories of resistance and oppression.
- Recognition of sexuality and the importance of experiences from early childhood.
- Recognition of the Oedipal complex.

DOI: 10.4324/9781003403920-17

The function of testimony in therapy, by the therapist and the patient, does not contradict any one of these Freudian principles. Undoubtedly, when the function of testimony is part of a general array of therapy, the therapeutic process is more complete. However, if because of conditions created in the clinic, the analytic therapy mostly leans on the position of the therapist as witness, one has to view it as a psychoanalytic therapy in the full sense of the word. All the more so, when it is known already that in every listening there exists an interpretation.

Possible Criticism or What Has Not Been Checked

One subject not checked and should be, is the connection between the emotional state of a person who does not feel that he had a caring witness in his life, or does not feel he/she has, and the inclination to suicide.

A further issue which has not been investigated is the link between the increasing search for witnesses for every experience and event they go through and their ongoing feeling of growing up alone.

In a non-representative series of interviews held with a number of youngsters who comment the day's events on social media platforms, a repetitive claim appears in their childhood: They were alone a great deal of the time, and the only friend they had was the cellular, the computer and the social network. What they feel is that their caretakers are/were not witnesses to their lives so that their use of social media is a backup form of acquiring witnesses.

Another possible criticism: By his very nature a person is homo-hermeneutics,[3] and the question arises as to what being a witness means?

Is being a witness an act of sacredness as in the Christian tradition, according to which the holy one is a witness who is not involved in 'normal' life and is always in the position of an observer?

And to what extent can an individual actually suspend the instinct to interpret?

If, indeed, interpretation is an inherent element in a person, then to place oneself in a position in which interpretation is suspended for a period of time, then there is in this, a dimension of overcoming an instinct[4] which turns the space of suspension in the position of witnessing into an arena of an inner struggle and to a dialectic space of overcoming a natural tendency.

Epilogue

The narrative of spoken testimony is fascinating.

Spoken testimony, that was perceived as a tool intended to complete, validate and shed light on an unclear reality, has been recognized towards the end of the 20th century as a medium of healing.

The attitude to spoken testimony changed in a 'natural' way, and except Elie Weisel, who confirmed that the *Two key events during the 20th century that are responsible for the highly important status of testimony in today's world are The Shoah and the development of psychoanalysis*, there was almost no philosophical or psychological preoccupation justifying or resisting its new ethical or moral value.

And so, testimony and trauma were bound together.

But, even from this bond, the act of testimony was saved and its important contributions to our lives became recognized in other aspects.

Following that, another surprising turn in the narrative testimony and witnessing happened, and this is the widespread phenomenon, expressed extensively in the social media. People of all ages, across cultural and social spectrum, are looking for witnesses to the events that take place in their lives.

The main key words of testimony and witnessing are being present and trust. Every testimony is a certificate of being present, but the healing power is based on trust.

Being present, from this point of view, is 'to be with'. There are here two kinds of 'to be': that of being with the other and that of a person being with himself.

This is not 'simple' trust, but rather a trust that comes with attention and careful listening, that grants the testifier validation and recognition.

The word 'testimony' has a double meaning: to give testimony and to witness the given testimony. The mutual relations between them creates a verbal and non-verbal emotional dialectic, which succeeds in holding the two sides and acts as a whole.

We need to remember that in each testimony there are at least three testimonies: There is the testimony that describes the experience endured by the narrator; there is the testimony that has been received by the addressee, which by definition differs from the testimony of the addresser; and there is the internal testimony that no one other than the testifier himself knows, and no other person feels it.

There is no such thing as a common space of suffering, as Tolstoy phrased it in "Anna Karenina": "Each unhappy family is unhappy in her own way". In order for the received testimony to be as close as possible to the given testimony, we have 'to be there', which means to turn to the patient and be attentive.

The word that constantly hovers over any testimony is attention
I like to end with a Zen anecdote which illustrates the wisdom of attention.

One day a man of the people said to Zen Master Ikkyu: "Master, will you please write for me some maxims of the highest wisdom?"
Ikkyu immediately took his brush and wrote the word "Attention".
"Is that all?" asked the man. "Will you not add something more?"
Ikkyu then wrote twice running: "Attention. Attention".
"Well," remarked the man rather irritably, "I really don't see much depth or subtlety in what you have just written."
Then Ikkyu wrote the same word three times running:
Attention. Attention. Attention.
Half agreed, the man demanded: "What does that word Attention mean anyway?"
And Ikkyu answered gently: "**Attention means Attention**."

List of References and Notes

1 Orange, Donna (1995): *Emotional Understanding: Studies in Psychoanalytic Epistemology*. The Guilford Press, New York & London, p. 137.
2 Freud, Sigmond (1923): Two Encyclopedia Articles: *The Standard Edition of the Complete Psychological Works of Sigmund Freud*, Volume XVIII (1920–1922): *Beyond the Pleasure Principle*, Group Psychology and Other Works, Hogarth Press in London, England, in 1953–1974, pp.233–260.
3 Sagi, Avi (2009): *The Human Voyage to Meaning*. Bar Ilan Press, Ramat Gan, Israel (Hebrew).
4 In this context another question arises, as to whether to call it an instinct or a drive.

Index

For Product Safety Concerns and Information please contact our EU
representative GPSR@taylorandfrancis.com
Taylor & Francis Verlag GmbH, Kaufingerstraße 24, 80331 München, Germany

9 7 8 1 0 3 2 5 1 7 8 0 3